D1060221

THE
EYE-VOICE
SPAN

THE
EYE-VOICE
SPAN

Harry Levin
with
Ann Buckler Addis

The MIT Press
Cambridge, Massachusetts,
and London, England

This book was set in VIP Times Roman by Grafacon, Inc., and
printed and bound by The Murray Printing Company in the
United States of America

Library of Congress Cataloging in Publication Data

Levin, Harry, 1925–
    The eye-voice span.

    Bibliography: p.
    Includes index.
    1. Reading, Psychology of. I. Addis, Ann Buckler.
II. Title.
BF456.R2L4823   153   79-19791
ISBN 0-262-12076-3

For Jackie and Jimmy Gibson

CONTENTS

Preface
ix

1
Introduction
1

2
The History of Methods for Measuring the EVS
7

3
Reading Silently and Aloud
19

4
Characteristics of the Text
39

5
Characteristics of the Reader
47

6
Telegraphy, Typewriting, and Music
69

7
Grammar, Meaning, and the EVS
81

8
The EVS and Types of Sentences
109

Notes
149

References
151

Index
163

PREFACE

My first interests in the eye-voice span began far from my home university, Cornell. In London I talked with Professor Frieda Goldman Eisler about pauses in oral reading as extensions of the excellent work she had done on pauses in speech, which had influenced some of my earlier research. Then, in Jerusalem I met Professor Itzhac Schlesinger who had just finished his thesis on grammar and reading in which he had used the eye-voice span. I was intrigued by the procedure and fretted during the rest of my trip abroad, because I wanted to try out this method as a way of studying the relationships between the grammatical structure of the text and reading. This was part of a larger program concerning the reading process. Initially, this research was funded by the National Institute of Mental Health (NIMH) and the National Science Foundation (NSF) and, ultimately, through the U.S. Office of Education's Project Literacy.

The listing of one's many coworkers seems trite until one

has the experience of doing research in a program that involves students and colleagues. Simply stated, the research could not be done without them. I hope I provided an opportunity for them to learn something about psychological research; I know I learned a great deal from them, and their many contributions are described in this book. I especially want to thank Ann Buckler Addis whose help in the preparation of the volume was invaluable and is acknowledged by her place on the title page. Other colleagues and students who made important contributions to the research program are Mary Beckwith, Andrew Biemiller, Elizabeth Turner Carswell, Julie Cohn, Boyce Ford, Jean Grossman, Dalton Jones, Eleanor Kaplan, Stanley Wanat, Rose-Marie Weber, and Raymond Wang. I thank all of them and often look back fondly to our partnership in research on reading.

The preparation of this report was delayed for a number of years. The duties of being a dean left little time for professional writing. I am grateful to my wife and children who treated my deanship with amused indulgence and did not let me forget that in their scheme of values, and my own, the primary job of the professor is to teach, to do research, and to write. I hope they are pleased that I have found my way back to the main road of their expectations. I certainly am.

I thank Roger Brown and Jeanne Chall for arranging a setting at Harvard University that made it easy for me to finish this book and to start a new program of research.

Finally, I am honored to dedicate this volume to James and Eleanor Gibson. They are good people, good friends, and models of the highest standards of our calling to their colleagues and to many generations of students.

Harry Levin

THE
EYE-VOICE
SPAN

1

INTRODUCTION

The eye-voice span (EVS) is the distance that the eye is ahead of the voice in reading aloud. The distance between the voice and the eyes is measured by time, letters, letter spaces, ems (a printer's measure), syllables, or words, which is the most common index. The EVS enjoys a long and useful history in the annals of educational and psychological research. Quantz (1897) was the first to publish a study on the EVS. Huey discussed the phenomenon in his important and foresighted book, *The Psychology and Pedagogy of Reading* (1908). Woodworth gave the EVS substantial coverage in 1938 in *Experimental Psychology*. A large-scale research program on the EVS was reported by Buswell in 1920, and we lean heavily on his excellent work.*

The EVS has been measured in only a few ways; the history of the methods are described in chapter 2. There are

---

* Readers may experience their own EVSs by starting now to read aloud

basically two empirical paradigms. In the simplest procedure, the one most often used in contemporary research, the subject reads a text aloud and at some predetermined point the text is made unavailable by covering it, removing it, or turning off the light. The reader reports what he has seen beyond the word he was saying aloud—often called the "critical position"—when the text was removed. The other method, which was used extensively before 1930 and only occasionally thereafter, involves the simultaneous measurement of the reader's eye movements and voice. The second method yields more detail and was appropriate when researchers were interested in the detailed "anatomy" of the EVS.

As may be expected, the popularity of each method was related to the interest in the EVS then dominant. The focus has changed during the eighty years that the phenomenon has been studied. At first, it was a curiosity to be described. Then, researchers became concerned with what the EVS could reveal about the reader: its relation to the reader's general reading skill or age. Such information made the EVS a useful tool for individual educational diagnosis, though there were unfortunate digressions when readers were trained to develop long EVSs under the mistaken belief that this would improve reading. There was actually some early concern with the ways that the reading materials influenced the EVS: the kind of type, the complexity of the text, or the reader's position on the line. The most recent interest in the EVS reflects the psychologists' and educators' attempts to understand the *process* of reading. This concern has been translated into many studies in which the text is varied in

---

and observing that they turn the page before their voices reach the last word on the page.

systematic ways in accordance with our increased sophistication in describing the grammatical and semantic natures of
written materials. Such topics are treated in the second half
of this book, and, if we may venture a prediction, future research on the EVS will reflect our growing knowledge about
how to analyze texts and, in turn, to ask how such materials
are read by different readers.

Said another way, the first researchers were interested in
the EVS itself. More recently, they have used the EVS as
one of several indicators as to the nature of the reading
process.

Almost from the first it was recognized that most readers'
EVSs varied from task to task. A reader does not carry
around an EVS of fixed size as characteristic as the color of
his eyes. Rather, the EVS operates like an accordion, bel-
lowing in or out for different parts of the same text. The
fundamental research goals, then, are to find out what
creates the changes. Though answers to these questions are
not now complete, and probably never will be, we can state
some things that the EVS is not.

The EVS is not simply guesses about the text beyond the
word being read aloud. EVSs may be as long as eight or ten
words. The likelihood is remote that readers are able to
guess correctly eight words in order. Besides, a direct test of
guessing indicated that adult readers make such guesses at
the rate of about one word per thousand (Levin and Kaplan
1968).

The voice and eyes are close to each other, but the eyes
pick up cues about upcoming words in peripheral vision. The
studies measuring both the voice and eye movements show

that the eyes are in advance of the voice. In addition, recent research on peripheral vision in reading indicates that only a limited number of words can be seen in the area of the fovea (clear vision) and that peripheral cues such as word length, word shapes, and first letters are inadequate to reproduce the string of words making up the EVS (McConkie and Rayner 1975).

What is Reading?
Ultimately, our interest in the EVS is the knowledge that this particular reading behavior has given us about the general processes of reading. Therefore, we will make clear what we believe reading to be and what principles govern reading behavior. This point of view informs our choice of materials covered in this book, their organization and interpretation, especially in the later chapters, which emphasize our own research.

Reading is extracting information from text.[1] Reading is an active process, self-directed by the reader in many ways and for many purposes. Some active approaches are as follows:

1. A flexibility of attentional strategies (at least for mature readers) in reading for different types of information.

2. A shift of strategy with characteristics of a text, such as difficulty of concepts and style.

3. A shift of strategy with rate of gain of knowledge as the reader progresses (e.g., he slows down under some circumstances, skims under others).

4. A shift of strategy with new or old information.

5. A shift of strategy with the reader's personal interests, his educational objectives, and with instructions.

In the development of reading there is a trend toward economy of processing:

1. The reader will direct his attention to processing textual material in the most economical way he can.

(a) The information relevant to the reader's purpose is selected for priority of attention.
(b) Information that is irrelevant, not wanted, or not useful for the task is ignored.
(c) The largest units appropriate for the task are processed. A reader can attend to features of letters, words, phrases, and even clauses as units.
(d) The least amount of information compatible with the reader's task is processed.

2. Adaptive reading is characterized by continual reduction of information.

(a) Processing is reduced in proportion to the number of alternatives that could follow in the ensuing information as the reader proceeds through the text.
(b) Alternatives are reduced by the application of rules and constraints.
(c) Alternatives are reduced by using old information to comprehend new information.

These principles of the reading process apply to the EVS, and in the concluding chapter the findings about EVSs will be summarized in light of these principles.

The Plan of This Book

Early researchers on the EVS often recorded eye movements and voices by ingenious electromechanical devices; the measurements are now simple to carry out by electronic technology. Nevertheless, the early findings still hold up well, and the basic empirical paradigms have remained the same throughout the history of research on the EVS. The early methodologies and research designs are the subjects of chapter 2. The EVS involves reading aloud. Our interests in reading, however, are directed to silent reading, and in chapter 3 we compare oral and silent reading in order to decide to what extent one may generalize between the two. Chapter 4 takes up some characteristics of the text: typography, line position, and languages other than English. Next, we focus on certain characteristics of readers as they influence the EVSs: age, reading skill, reading rate, etc.

Telegraphy, typewriting, and reading music have certain characteristics in common with reading aloud, and spans on those tasks are discussed in chapter 6. The two final chapters are devoted to what we consider the most important research on the EVS: the effects of grammatical structure and meaning.

2

THE
HISTORY
OF
METHODS
FOR
MEASURING
THE EVS

There are two basic ways to measure the EVS, and both
were used early in the course of research on this topic. The
first and simplest method is to remove the text from the person reading aloud and to record the material the person is
able to repeat after removal of the text. The other method
involves simultaneously recording eye movements and the
voice and coordinating the two records. The simpler method
has had minor opportunities for technical improvement; the
second grew from ingenious contraptions to sophisticated
technological improvements in measuring eye movements
and recording sound.

Formal research on the EVS started with Quantz's study
in 1897. Quantz slipped a card over the text when the subject's voice reached certain predetermined points, recorded
the number of words pronounced after the interference, and
called the score the "eye-voice separation." The subjects
were not told the purpose of the experiment, so the card

blocking the book must have been a surprise. Quantz did not find the first trial's results significantly different from those of later trials.

Huey (1898) made several observations akin to the EVS without using any overt interventions. "By having the subject read aloud and noting the syllable pronounced just as the eye turned for the return sweep, I found that I could get the approximate distance of the eye ahead of pronunciation, for at least one point in the line" (p. 583). Huey's alternative method (1908) was to wait for the reader to turn the page and see how many words were left to pronounce from the previous page.

Beginning in 1917, more sophisticated and elaborate methods were devised to locate the eyes and the voice during oral reading. Gray (1917), who thought that Quantz's method was crude, developed the apparatus diagramed in figure 2.1. Since the apparatus was used in a number of research projects, it may be useful to describe it in some detail. The "Rube Goldberg" quality of the apparatus was clever, and, surprisingly, we have not improved a great deal on the findings from eye-movement studies by modern, refined, computerized equipment.

The source of light was an arc lamp under rheostat control. The light passed through a double convex lens and a cooling tank, then focused on a small hole in a diaphragm that cut off all marginal light. One prong of a tuning fork, vibrating at the rate of fifty per second, was placed between the lamp and the diaphragm so that the light was chopped every fiftieth of a second, thus providing a time record for the eventual photograph of eye movements. As the light diverged after the diaphragm, it was passed through a second

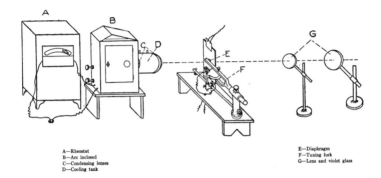

A—Rheostat
B—Arc inclosed
C—Condensing lenses
D—Cooling tank

E—Diaphragm
F—Tuning fork
G—Lens and violet glass

2.1
Apparatus for measuring eye
movements (Gray 1917).

convex lens that broke it up into a series of parallel rays. To reduce its intensity, the light was filtered through violet glass and passed to two mirrors, the second of which reflected the light into the reader's eyes. Light reflected from the eyes entered a camera lens so that any movement of the eyes changed the direction of light that was recorded on a moving film.

Selections of text to be read were projected to a surface below the camera, where they could be seen by the reader-subject. Oral reading was recorded on an Edison dictaphone. Each revolution of the wax cylinder briefly closed a shutter put into the beam of light and rang a bell that was recorded on the dictaphone. The break in light on the film and the bell on the cylinder could be synchronized to give the EVS.

One of Gray's records is reproduced in figure 2.2. The lengths of the vertical lines are proportional to the durations of the fixations. Notice, for example, that this subject fixated

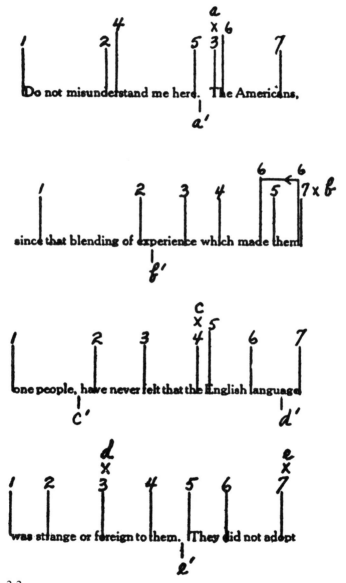

2.2
Location of one reader's eye-
movement fixations and eye-
voice span in oral reading (Gray
1917).

point 4 longer than point 2. The numbers above the lines give the sequence of fixations. This reader fixated points 1 and 2 in order, moved to 3, then went back to 4 and 5. The EVS is read as "when the voice is at a', the eyes are at a; voice at b', eyes at b; etc." This subject showed spans of varying size within the passage: the eye and voice were almost together at the end of a sentence and quite far apart even when going from one line to another, d' to d. Such records were useful for studying eye movements during oral reading as well as for measuring the separation between the eyes and the voice.

With the addition of a better calibrated light source, Buswell (1920) carried out extensive and informative studies of the EVS. One of his records is reproduced in figure 2.3. The reader is a fourth grader who was, according to Buswell, a poor reader. The numbers at the top of the vertical lines give the order of fixations; those at the bottom, the length of fixations in fiftieths of seconds. The voice and eye are labeled clearly. Buswell closed the shutter at systematic, predetermined points in the text. This record shows instances of the EVS at beginnings, middles, and ends of lines.

Tiffin's (1934) experimental arrangement took advantage of the various technical advances available between 1930 and 1934. Voices were recorded by a commercial cutter for recording aluminum disc phonograph records. An oscillograph record of the amplitude of the voice was recorded on the same film as the eye movements. Although this device did not record waveforms very accurately, it adequately located various words and syllables of the selection. An improved version of Tiffin's equipment is diagramed in figure 2.4.

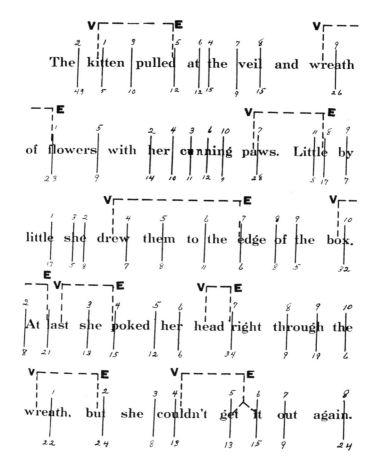

2.3
EVS of one fourth-grade subject, poor reader (Buswell 1920).

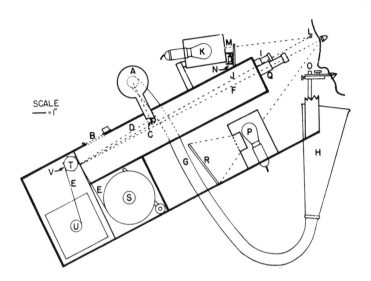

Fig. 1. Schematic drawing of the eye-voice camera. A, phonelescope; B, focusing window; C, mirror; D, beam of light from phonelescope; E, film; F, beam of light from eye; G, speaking tube; H, horn; I, head-line lens; J, beam of light for head-line; K, source of light for head-line; L, bead on spectacle frames; M, point of time line interruption; N, 60 cycle vibrator; O, jaw rest; P, eye and reading material light source; Q, eye lens; R, reading material; S, film supply spool; T, film sprocket; U, film take-up box; V, motor shaft.

2.4
Schematic of eye-voice camera
(Tiffin and Fairbanks 1937).

A final improvement in eye-movement photography for purposes of studying the EVS was reported by Geyer (1966, 1969). Basically, the method differed little from Tiffin and Fairbanks (1937). The apparatus consisted of a Gilbert eye-movement camera modified to synchronize eye-movement data with the voice records. The voice records were made on a tape recorder and played through a polygraph that accurately measured elapsed time.

Geyer recognized that corneal reflections were less accurate than previously thought and carefully calibrated the eye movements to compensate for the less than perfect spherical shape of the cornea. All researchers who photographically recorded eye movements were aware of the problems of keeping the head immobile. Chin rests and head clamps of various designs were used, none completely satisfactory. When the head was sufficiently restrained, the subject was in an uncomfortable, unnatural position. Independent reflections from the head—the so-called ''head lines''—were used to correct eye position for the movements of the head, but this was not understood well and added little to the accuracy of measurement.

Another methodological approach to the measurement of eye movements involves electrooculography (Morton, 1964b). This method uses the difference in potential between the front and the back of the eyeball. The field from this dipole moves as the eyeball rotates; electrodes on the skin detect changes in the potential, and these are amplified and recorded on paper as a continuous record. (Figure 2.5 shows Morton's diagram of his experimental arrangement.) A second channel of the pen recorder records impulses from a throat microphone. A tape recording of the voice is also made. Because of electronic noise in the system, Morton reported that it was necessary to reject some of the records.

Recent research on the EVS resurrected Quantz's simple procedure. It will be recalled the Quantz made the text

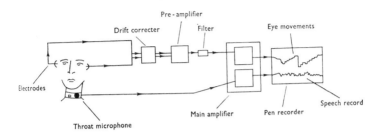

2.5
EVS apparatus, using electrooculography (Morton 1964b).

unavailable at some points and then recorded the words of
the text that the readers were able to report beyond those
points. In the midst of his eye-movement research, Buswell
(1937) used that simple method. He was trying to train a
class to develop wider EVSs. Paragraphs were projected on
a screen, and the class was told to read aloud. At predetermined points the lights were extinguished, and EVSs were
measured.

There are many ways to remove the text while the subject
is reading. Levin and Turner (1968; Rode 1974–1975) exposed the text in a box covered with one-way, mirrored
glass. The text was visible when the light in the box was on.
The experimenter operated the light by a microswitch that
simultaneously operated a timer so that reading speed could
be measured.

In an even simpler method the texts were prepared on
slides that were shown on a ground-glass rear projection
screen. The screen was placed so that the subject could read

with little head movement; the size of the letters on the screen was approximately the same as in standard texts. Subjects fixated on a point at the upper-left corner of the screen, about where the selection would begin when projected. This helped the subject to begin reading immediately without perusing the text before starting to read aloud. Each slide included a single light-out position. The experimenter closed the shutter at a predetermined point, and the reader was asked to repeat as much of the text beyond the light-off position as he could recall. Written or taped records were made of the readers' responses. Among the researchers using this method were Lawson (1961), Levin and Kaplan (1968), Schlesinger (1968), Resnick (1970), and Bond and Tinker (1973).

This method calls for the experimenter to practice placing the light-out position accurately. The experimenter's personal reaction time can introduce variability in the points where the text is removed. We have found that when the experimenter pushes the light-off switch during the interword interval between the target word and the one prior to it, the reaction time is such that the subject will be saying the target word. When the experimenter waits for the reader to start the critical word, light-off is at critical word plus one.

The two methods of measuring the EVS represent different research purposes and strategies. A useful demarcation date between earlier and later EVS research is 1960. The earlier work was carried out in the context of understanding the nature of eye movements during reading and relating eye movements to characteristics of the reader. The records were continuous and complete so that researchers could reconstruct EVSs according to positions in the line; they often were content to report the existence of spans and their variations among readers. The post-1960 research was more clearly focused on grammatical or semantic characteristics of the text, approximations to English, and so forth. Said another way, the earlier research concentrated on the nature of eye movements; the later, on the nature of the text.

READING
SILENTLY
AND
ALOUD

Reading is a private process. The consequences of reading, such as memory or comprehension of the text, are readily available, but information about the ongoing process of reading is hard to obtain. The measurement of eye movements is the most obvious and the most thoroughly studied component of the reading process. Electromyography of the speech musculature during silent reading has been carried out, but the relationships between implicit vocalizations and reading are obscure.

The issue is important because the EVS is based on oral reading. Oral reading—reading aloud—is easily arranged and observed, but researchers and practitioners are usually interested in oral reading as observable behavior that may provide information about the process of silent reading. The essential question, then, concerns the nature of the relationships between oral and silent reading. If these relationships are obscure, complex, or nonexistent, interest in oral reading pales. If the two modes of reading are similar and their similarities and differences are understandable, our interest in oral reading is justified. The intention of this chapter is to review and evaluate the research that has compared oral and silent reading. The two modes of reading will be compared on the following topics: (1) nature of the text; (2) characteristics of the readers; (3) eye movements; (4) reading speed; and (5) comprehension and memory.

This summary paraphrases Anderson and Dearborn (1952). On one side are investigators such as Judd, Buswell, and Cole, who see the two modes as involving different processes. They emphasize differences in eye movements and reading speeds. Other investigators, such as Anderson and Dearborn, Rogers, Swanson, and Fairbanks, believe the processes are similar and, while accepting the eye-movement findings, dwell on the similarities of silent and oral reading. Those who read well in one mode do so in the other. Comprehension is similar as is the development of the skills. Anderson and Dearborn conclude that silent and oral reading may be implicit and overt expressions, respectively, of the same underlying processes. This chapter will be devoted to understanding that assertion.

The Nature of the Text
Judd's (1918) study was the only one that compared how oral and silent reading are affected by typographic variations: the size of type. Three adult readers, two skilled and one poor reader, read text printed in normal-sized type and type that was twice as large and half as large as normal. Negligible differences in eye movements during silent and oral reading were attributable to the physiognomic variations

of the text. The results reinforced Judd's belief that reading in the two modes is similar and that the distance the eyes span is more dependent on the person's "central processing" than the physical characteristics of the visual display.

There has been much conjecture and some research on the ways that the grammatical and meaning structure of the text influence oral and silent reading. The earlier interest was devoted to learning how the two modes created different conditions for taking advantage of the structures that exist in the text. Accordingly, Clark (1915) and Bond and Tinker (1973) believed that in both modes reading must occur in "thought units," which facilitate comprehension by organizing material into logical phrases.

Judd (1918), Gray (1925), and Tinker (1965; references made therein to an earlier report) distinguish the two reading modes precisely on the nature of the units they induce. In oral reading because some attention must be given to making the sounds (to the articulatory mechanisms), the units may be speech units, that is, words. In silent reading attention does not have to be divided between the eye and the voice, so undivided attention can be given to meaning. The units can be larger and more meaningful, that is, phrase units.

Readers who move the lips in silent reading lose the advantage of rapid fusion of words into ideas which is made possible by focussing the attention entirely on the substance of the material being read without any obligation to pronounce the words either orally or to one's self. (Buswell 1937, p. 87)

Notice that the implication in Buswell's writing is that units are built or fused rather than extracted or reorganized, two points of view that are extensively discussed by Gibson and Levin (1975).

Wanat (1971) reported a detailed analysis of eye movements of persons reading several types of grammatical constructions silently and aloud. The reading of right- and left-embedded sentences were compared (*The sculptor carved the chapel which was extraordinarily detailed* vs. *The sculptor who was very skilled carved the chapel*). For all sentence types oral reading required greater amounts of visual attention, took more time, and needed a larger number of fixations than silent reading. The two modes of reading did not differ on various kinds of visual regressions.

Wanat also compared the silent and oral reading of active (*The boy hit the ball*) and passive (*The ball was hit by the boy*) sentences. Reading aloud required more visual attention, as indexed by the amount of time spent on each sentence and the number of forward fixations, but the differences between oral and silent reading as described above tended to be similar for all sentence types. Regressive eye movements were different, however, for active and passive sentences. The regressions were most marked in the agent deleted passives (*The ball was hit by the park*). There were more regressions for this type of passive sentence, but the differences occurred only in oral reading. In summary, the eye movements on all sentence types were similar in silent reading, but regressions were more marked in the oral mode for certain kinds of passive sentences. There is no simple or obvious explanation for these findings.

The two reading modes have been compared for various languages. Ai (1950) reported that among the Chinese by the fifth and sixth grades silent reading was superior by about one word per second. Gray (1958) summarized findings from studies of various languages carried out by others, as well as his own comparisons of fourteen languages. Results from France and Germany showed that from about the fourth grade on silent is faster than oral reading.

In Chinese (Hu 1928) fiction was read aloud at the rate of about 3.7 words per second and silently at 5 words per second; nonfictional prose at 3.7 and 4.2 words per second; and poetry at 2.9 and 3.4 words per second. Similar results are true for Japanese. The results from writing systems that contain ideographic elements must be compared cautiously, if at all, to alphabetic systems (Gibson and Levin 1975). More detailed comparisons of poetry would be interesting, since certain types of poetry are designed to be read aloud, using stress, rhythm, and rhyme in ways that should facilitate oral reading. The small amount of information we have suggests that poetry is read more slowly than prose, in both modes.

As may be expected, there were language-to-language variations among Gray's fourteen languages, though some consistencies were notable. Comprehension scores after oral and silent reading were found to be about equal in all cases. The durations of visual fixations were longer during oral than silent reading in all languages, but the average number of words recognized per fixation varied among the languages. For English and French the span of recognition (fixation to fixation) was larger in silent reading; in Korean the oral mode was larger. For the others the two spans were similar. There were more regressions during oral reading for all languages but Korean and Burmese. We note again that these findings are difficult to explain without reflections on the nature of the writing systems. Gray asserts that the number of regressions was not affected by the language's orthography, topographical variations (such as printing text without spaces between words), or the number of words needed to express an idea. He cites these reasons for regressions in oral reading: (1) in addition to other reasons, there are the same reasons that exist in silent reading; (2) regressions permit the reader to check his pronunciation and the order of words; (3) regressions allow the reader to determine the correct inflections; and (4) regressions allow the voice to catch up to the eye.

Gray concludes that surface characteristics of the text have little influence on oral-silent reading. Rather, the differences are due to ways in which reading has been learned (the Hebrew and Arabic readers reported that they had been taught to pay detailed attention to the text) and to the "syntactic-semantic" characteristics of the text. In summary, one can say that although the relationships differ somewhat from one language to the next, except for comprehension, silent reading is the more efficient of the two modes.

Characteristics of the Readers

Ages

In this section we will review the development of oral and silent reading in people of various ages. Pintner and Gilliland (1916) devised a score—the reading value—to compare the two modes of reading. The reading value is the number of correct ideas recalled after reading a passage, divided by the number of seconds it took to read the selection, a sort of piece of idea per second. Taking apart the components of the ratio, the high school and college students read silently faster than orally. The other grades showed no differences. "This would seem to suggest that increase in rapidity of reading comes relatively late and that with children silent reading differs from oral reading merely in the fact that the words are not pronounced aloud and there may be in this silent reading almost as much articulation as in oral reading'' (p. 204).

The number of ideas reproduced was about equal for both types of reading in all groups. Silent reading led to substantially higher ''reading values'' for college students and high schoolers. Among the younger students, the silent-oral differences were trivial or nonexistent.

Most researchers report that in the early grades the rates of reading silently and aloud are similar or that oral is faster (Oberholtzer 1915; Stone 1922; Gray 1925; Cole 1938; Ai 1950). Oberholtzer believed that oral superiority is due to young children's dependence on sound for comprehension. Because of variations in materials and methods, it is not surprising that there is little agreement about the age at which the rate of silent reading surpasses oral. Judd (1918) thought that a child's silent reading resembles an adult's reading aloud. The implication is reasonable in that oral reading requires the adult to attend to smaller units of text, which is characteristic of a child's reading in both modes.

In spite of their agreement that reading rate is similar in both modes for young children, researchers diverge widely about the grade level at which children begin to read silently more quickly: end of the first or beginning of the second grade (Cole 1938); in the third grade (Stone 1922); in the fourth grade (Ai 1950); or in the second to the fourth grade (Gray 1925). At some deviance from the above findings, Pintner and Gilliland (1916) report that the differences in rate did not occur until high school. ''This would seem to suggest that increase in rapidity of reading comes relatively late and that with children silent reading differs from oral reading merely in the fact that the words are not pronounced aloud and there may be in this silent reading *almost as much articulation as in oral reading*" (p. 204, our emphasis).

The developmental curves of reading rate show the crossover points of the two modes; eye-movement records provide the basic data. Researchers report similar courses of development of the recognition span (saccade length) for oral and silent reading. There is rapid growth in length of "span" until the fourth grade, a plateau until the middle of high school, and then another, smaller increase in saccade length (Buswell 1920; Stone 1922; Gray 1925). The curves for both reading modes are similar, with oral reading below silent reading. "The principal significance of a comparison of the oral and silent curves lies in the fact that throughout the grades, at least above the first, the silent-reading process makes possible or stimulates broader recognition units, while in oral reading the use of these wide fixations is inhibited. ". . . In oral reading some attention must be given to each word as it is pronounced" (Buswell 1922, p. 39).

The growth in regularity of eye movements, as measured by the number of regressions per line, is similar for oral and silent reading (Stone 1922; Gray 1925). There was a rapid increase in regularity through the fourth grade. The regularity was greater for silent reading, and the differences between the two modes increased with age.

To understand the pedagogical implications that were drawn from the studies of eye movements while reading aloud or silently, one must understand the importance attached to eye movements in the twenties. Because skilled readers exhibited smooth eye movements, training in moving one's eyes while reading was thought to be critical in learning to read. Hence, if oral reading showed some benign forms of eye movements, reading aloud was applauded as a necessary skill for mature reading. The following statement is more or less typical: "until the child has reached a certain stage of maturity in reading habits, the development of fluency in oral reading is an aid in establishing good eye movements" (Stone 1922, p. 16). A more modern counterargument states that oral reading, which is usually taught first in school, hinders the more efficient mode of reading at a later time (McDade 1941).

Reading Skill and Oral and Silent Reading
Do people who read well aloud read well silently? Most investigators report that those who do well in one mode of reading also do well in the other. Gray's (1916) statement is characteristic: "A careful study of individual records shows clearly that those pupils who are able to move forward quickly in oral reading are the pupils who read most rapidly silently" (p. 184). Swanson (1937) did the most thorough study of this question. His subjects, 70 poor silent readers and 10 good silent readers, were selected on the basis of their scores on the Iowa Silent Reading Test. The correlation between the oral comprehension and silent comprehension scores by which the groups were selected indicates once more that readers remember equally well from both modes. There was little difference in the rate of oral reading between good and poor silent readers. Poor silent readers made more oral reading errors than the more skilled group.

This study was elaborated by Anderson and Swanson (1937). The eye movements during oral and silent reading were compared for these groups: poor, unselected, and good readers. The patterns of eye movements were most similar for the poor readers, less similar for the unselected group, and most dissimilar for the good readers. The authors conclude, "It follows that the central processes occurring in the two types of reading are more intimately related in poor readers than in average or good readers" (p. 63). If by "central processes" the authors mean general ability, it is not surprising that poor silent readers do poorly in many intellectual tasks. Also, the difference between good and poor readers was greatest for silent reading, because the demands of oral reading, such as articulation rate, put a ceiling on performance for both groups. Further, poor readers may still be using oral reading habits in their silent reading, thus exaggerating the similarity in performance in the two modes.

Jones and Lockhart (1919) inadvertently demonstrated a substantial correlation between oral and silent reading. They drew four groups—a *small* group which performed well orally, but poorly on the silent test; a *large* group that did well on both; a *large* group that performed poorly on both; and a *small* group that did well on the silent test, but poorly on the oral one. This pattern of frequencies demonstrates a relationship between the two reading modes. The study, though, may be faulted on the tests used, which seemed to compare silent reading comprehension with oral reading pronunciation.

Early researchers characterized good and poor readers in terms of their "perception accuracy," but it is difficult to know what they meant by this archaic concept. Presumably they were saying that good readers are less bound by the text, whereas poor readers attend to small units (or words).

The ability to use larger-than-word units implies attention to meaning as a direct act of reading, the so-called use of "central processes." Good readers evidence higher degrees of perception accuracy in both silent and oral reading than poor readers.

Eye Movements during Oral and Silent Reading

Almost from the beginning, researchers on oral and silent reading regarded the recording and interpreting of eye movements as the most "scientific" method of studying the reading process. It is not surprising, therefore, that a number of scientists recorded eye movements during the two modes of reading. Their results are fairly consistent; there are more fixations in oral than in silent reading (Schmidt 1917; Judd 1918; O'Brien 1926). Buswell's (1937) explanation is reasonable: "Oral reading necessarily requires attention on each individual word since every word must be pronounced, whereas in silent reading certain words play a small part in the total composite meaning and may be passed over with only a small amount of attention" (p. 86).

Wanat's (1971) study of oral and silent reading of sentences with varied grammatical structure has already been described. Briefly, in reading right- and left-embedded sentences, oral reading required more fixations per line (2.8) than silent (2.6). Active and passive sentences also required more fixations in the oral than in the silent mode (2.4 and 2.1, respectively).

Researchers also found more regressions during oral reading (Schmidt 1917; Stone 1933; Gray 1925); these results were almost as consistent as those for fixations. Oral reading, being slower, may require more regressions in order to remember the earlier text. Also, regressions provide information about appropriate sentence intonation and allow the voice to catch up with the eyes.

Wanat (1971) separated the regressions by sentence types and eye movements. He reported no differences in regressions for left- and right-embedded sentences read silently or aloud. Oral reading of active and passive sentences did not require more refixations and regressions, but more *time* was spent on regressions. This finding is particularly marked in agent-deleted passives (*The ball was hit by the park*). The reading regression times on such sentences was twice that for oral reading on all other sentences, and several times the amount required for silent reading. Agent-deleted passives also required more regressions.

Wanat offered several explanations, none of them entirely satisfactory, for the longer regression times in oral reading. The less constrained locative form (*by the park*) must be given an intonation pattern different from the one appropriate for an agentive by-phrase. This sequence, however, would require more processing time, not more regressive eye movements. A second solution is that the auditory form gives the reader further information that the word after *by* is not the expected word. This explanation implies that when there were no regressions the conflict was not detected and the word was incorrectly identified and read. There is the further implication that there were many misreadings in silent reading, a conjecture not borne out by comprehension tests. Wanat concludes that different modes of reading different forms require different allocations of visual attention. The conclusion is certainly as true as it is unsatisfying.

Buswell (1920), in his classic research on the EVS, varied

the text in ways that provide analogous data to Wanat's. He studied eye movements during oral and silent reading of paragraphs containing words that may be pronounced in several ways depending on the context. An example of such a sentence is "She had tears in her dress and also tears in her eyes" (p. 87). Characteristic eye movements accompanied any difficulties and were the same for both oral and silent reading. "This shows that eye movements in both oral and silent reading are largely controlled by the recognition of meaning" (Buswell 1920, p. 99).

One final comment about eye movements. Anderson and Swanson (1937) report that the differences in eye movements between the two modes of reading increase with reading ability. They also increase, at least slightly, with age and school grade.

The findings of "attention spans" or "spans of recognition" in oral and silent reading are analogous to the eye-movement results, since they are derived from the number and pattern of fixations. Stated simply, fewer fixations per unit of text is interpreted as longer spans. All authors report narrower spans in oral reading. Judd (1918) wrote, "In oral reading the eye moves from word to word, directing in this way the vocal apparatus as it utters each unit. . . . If the mind can grasp a phrase, that becomes the unit governing fixation" (p. 21). Cole (1938), on the other hand, assumes that the eye is always with the voice in oral reading and that the units of fixation are syllables. Cole's findings, since they fly in the face of much that we know about the EVS, seem unlikely.

Smith (1971), at least using more modern terminology, believes that the limit in oral reading is four or five words, the amount that will fill short-term memory. This same limit does not apply to silent reading, because the reader does not have to identify every word, the stimuli can be organized and stored in a more permanent form. In silent reading, then, short-term memory is not filled with individual letters or words, but with meanings. "If he [the reader] were able to fill his memory with meanings, he might well be responsive to dependencies extending over a dozen words or more" (p. 198). Chunking allows the reader to grasp meaningful segments and to store only their total meaning in short-term memory. This is not possible in oral reading, where readers must recall all the words they have seen.

As with eye movements, spans are wider in silent than in oral reading (Gray 1925). Good readers have larger spans in both reading modes (Tinker 1965), and the spans in both modes narrow when the reader encounters difficulties (Buswell 1920).

These findings are substantially confirmed even when other measurement methods for span sizes are used (Bouma and deVoogd 1974).

The higher span for silent reading found in the experiments probably indicates that silent reading proceeds less carefully in the sense that a lower proportion of words has to be identified as such . . . correct oral reading of text seems to require nearly perfect recognition of each individual word (reading for reproduction), whereas silent reading proceeds somewhat more loosely (reading for meaning). (p. 26)

Bouma and deVoogd believe that the spans are similar in both modes, that is, the number of words simultaneously available for processing, but that the silent span is not directly available for measurement.

The main findings of studies of eye movements during silent and oral reading are these: there are more fixations when reading aloud; the distances between fixations are longer when reading silently; and regressions during reading in both modes depend on the complexity of the text, though there tend to be more regressions during oral reading.

Rate of Reading

The literature comparing the rate of oral reading with that of silent reading is voluminous. All investigators report that silent is faster than oral reading (Quantz 1897; Huey 1908; Schmidt 1917; Gray 1925, 1958; Buswell 1937; Wanat 1971). Buswell claims that it is impossible to read more than 250 words per minute aloud or 600 words per minute silently. The differences in rate are universally explained by physiological factors. Huey (1908), for example, pointed out that oral reading, and speaking, can occur only on the expiration of breath, whereas silent reading, which early researchers thought involved inner speech, can occur during both expiration and inspiration. Judd (1916a) wrote that oral reading is limited by the speech musculature.

The rate limits imposed by the speech musculature occasionally reduced the difference in the speed of reading in one mode compared to another. Quantz (1897) found that if a reader moved his lips, his rate of silent reading would be low. The ten slowest readers in his group had almost double the amount of lip movements as the ten fastest readers in the study. Since the limits imposed by the vocal musculature are similar for all readers, the range of possible rates is much narrower for oral than for silent reading. Schmidt's (1917) summary is a propos:

The very marked differences which are in evidence in the case of some individuals indicate very clearly that it is possible to make much greater distinctions between the two types of reading than are ordinarily made. The rate of oral reading, although subject to considerable variation is confined within relatively narrow limits because of its dependence upon the physiological mechanism involved in vocalization. Silent reading, on the other hand, is much more independent of physiological factors, though by no means entirely so, since the great majority of readers are dependent upon the so-called inner speech of reading. (p. 82)

Memory and Comprehension after Oral and Silent Reading
Memory was usually measured as the readers' accuracy in reproducing the materials read; comprehension, the ability to answer questions about the text. Memory is certainly implicated in comprehension, whereas it is possible to reproduce by rote with little or no understanding.

Four of the five studies of memory used the same methods. Passages were analyzed by the number of "points," "thoughts," or "ideas" they contained. Equal numbers of passages were read silently and aloud. Pintner (1913) reported that the average number of points reproduced after oral reading was 15; after silent reading, 18. He claimed that the differences would have been larger, if the children had received some training in reading silently. Two additional studies yielded the same results (Mead 1915, 1917). Pintner and Gilliland (1917) found no differences between the two modes in the number of points remembered.

Memorizing poetry is a special kind of task. The results depend on whether the verse is to be recalled orally or in writing. Poetry provides the opportunity for the memorizer to use rhythm to chunk the text and rhyme to act as a mnemonic. Woody (1922) reported that memorization of poetry, as well as reading speed (contrary to results reported above), was superior with oral reading. However, the study should not be taken too seriously because of its questionable method of testing and the fact that those who performed well in one mode did so in the other, suggesting general ability effects.

Controversies over whether one understands text better during oral or silent reading have appeared in the literature for many years. Some conjectures about the superiority of oral reading include the belief that the added auditory stimulation aids comprehension. An obvious contrary hypothesis holds that the requirement of making sounds—attention to vocalizing—detracts from comprehension. The possibility of no differences is based on the assumption that comprehension depends on central rather than peripheral factors. Another finding-cum-hypothesis is that skilled readers better understand materials read silently, whereas poor readers profit from reading aloud, presumably because of the contribution of the second modality as well as the focused attention required by oral reading.

The wisdom of consensus was that attention paid to vocalizing detracted from the attention to understanding what was read. Jones and Lockhart (1919) concluded in the jargon of the times, "The necessary innervations to the vocal organs tend to inhibit the nerve currents stimulating thought processes. . . . The visual impression of the printed word sets off the speech reaction, but in doing so inhibits thought reactions" (p. 590). This point of view was generally shared

(Judd and Buswell 1922; Stone 1922; Gray 1925; O'Brien 1926; Buswell 1937; Cole 1938).

Overattention to articulation is most likely to occur where the nature of the test forces the subject to concentrate on enunciation and pronunciation. Buswell (1927) found a situation that most of us would agree requires extraordinary attention to articulation to the detriment of understanding. The subjects were instructed to read aloud and to understand a passage in a foreign language they were studying. To no one's surprise, the subjects said that they had paid attention to the pronunciation rather than the meaning of the text. It is difficult to know what generalizations to draw from Buswell's study.

More recent research (e.g., Gray 1958; Anderson and Swanson 1937; Swanson 1937) shows consistently that there is little difference in the comprehension of materials read orally and silently. Rogers (1937) reported no differences in comprehension after three experimental variations. First, subjects read for a fixed length of time; second, they read a fixed amount of material; and, third, they had various amounts of time during which to read. The very small superiority of silent reading evaporated when the readers had more time, but there was no progressive improvement with increases in time. "The notion that good but not poor readers are handicapped by oral reading because the latter have never relinquished their early habits is not supported by this research" (p. 397).

Poulton and Brown (1967) found no clear differences in comprehension and cogently question the belief that attention to vocalizing reduces comprehension. "But since reading aloud is a highly overlearnt skill, after approximately 150 words she was able to programme her [the reader's] vocal output satisfactorily. It could then continue to run with the minimum of attention, leaving her more free to concentrate upon storing the information in the passage" (p. 221).

Attacking the other supposed virtue of reading aloud—the bimodality practice through sound *and* vision—Smith (1971) emphasizes that the reader still must extract the meaning from the words. "The meaning of a language is no more given directly in its sound than it is available in the surface structure of writing" (p. 200). "There is another widespread misconception that spoken words have a kind of magical character; that their meaning is apparent the moment they are uttered" (p. 207).

The research on memory and comprehension, much of it carried out many years ago, does not give an equivocal picture of findings, though they are clearer than many other sections of this chapter. In testing memory, silent reading in most cases was superior to oral reading. One wonders, though, whether the results would have been different if oral memory tests followed oral reading. Early findings on comprehension favored silent reading, usually explained by the supposition that attention given to vocalization detracted from understanding the text. More recent research, generally more sophisticated, found no differences between the two modes on comprehension and concluded that the central processes underlying comprehension were similar in both types of reading.

The intention of this chapter, it will be recalled, was to summarize the similarities and differences between silent and oral reading with a view to studying the more available oral reading as a guide to the processes of silent reading. There are enough similarities to warrant attention to oral reading, although the two modes are different enough to suggest caution in extrapolating from one to the other. Anderson's and Dearborn's (1952) conclusion, although encouraging, is probably too optimistic: "The evidence suggests rather that silent and oral reading are significantly related and have many elements in common. An alternative hypothesis, therefore, is that oral and silent reading may be the overt and implicit expressions, respectively, of the same fundamental process" (p. 160).

What are the similarities? First, all of the curves plotting the development of reading skills for the two modes were parallel, though skill in silent reading developed more rapidly. Second, those readers who performed well in one mode also did well in the other. Third, memory for text was superior after silent reading, though text was understood equally well in both modes. Fourth, perception of text, as indexed by eye movements, was similar for both modes. More skilled readers used more efficient eye movements when reading either silently or aloud. Fifth, difficulties in reading material led to characteristic regressions, and sometimes what Buswell (1920) called confused eye movements, during both types of reading. Sixth, as was shown by the EVS studies, skilled readers processed the text in systematic or meaning units. Most investigators infer that the "idea," or "meaning unit," is operative in silent reading.

Therefore, reading in either mode involves the extraction of meaning from the text, and beyond the superficialities of vocalizing many of the findings hang together, if we assume that higher-order processes are similar for silent and oral reading.

4

CHARACTERISTICS
OF THE TEXT

Once the EVS phenomenon became apparent, the early researchers attended to its correlates. Certain variables were
obvious candidates. Characteristics of the readers—their
ability and age—were immediately related to the EVS,
whereas characteristics of the text, the most prevalent modern problem, yielded position on the line and in the sentence
as likely determinants of the EVS. To be sure, the early researchers did write about "units of thought" and "ideas" as
conditioning factors in the EVS, but the lack of appropriate
theories and units of analysis left these early harbingers of
interesting problems as merely vague statements.

Position on the Line
Quantz (1897), the EVS pioneer, wrote that the length of the
span varied regularly with the position on the line at which
the text was removed. Near the beginning of the line, the
average span was 7.4 words; at the middle of the line, 5.1

words; and at the end, 3.8 words. Such regularity was disrupted by unfamiliar words, which reduced the span, or familiar phrases, which increased it.

Huey (1908), in his concern with the motor habits of reading, summarized W. F. Dearborn. Dearborn believed that fast readers establish a regular, rhythmical eye-movement pattern during reading. This includes making a fixed number of pauses per line "independently of variations in subject matter from line to line" (p. 177) and establishing a uniform arrangement in the order of long and short pauses. He said that fixation points were fixed for every line, all lines having the same stopping points. The point itself could be any part of a word or the spacing between words, and paid "little attention to the rules of apperception or those of the rhetorician" (p. 47). These statements are a clear exposition of the motor theory of reading, which we now know to be wrong, but which was once influential. From this theory it follows that the EVS would depend on the position in the line, as Quantz had found. In fact short spans at line endings are not unreasonable, because the voice "catches up" with the eyes as they make the sweep from the end of one line to the beginning of the next.

Buswell (1920) investigated the effects of line position. He found that the EVSs were 12.7, 12.7, and 10.9 letter spaces at the beginning, middle, and end of the line, respectively. Note that these spans were considerably shorter than those Quantz measured for *words*. There is modest agreement with Quantz that the EVS is shorter at ends of lines, though the more reasonable reading of Buswell's findings is that the EVS is not influenced by line position. Buswell did find many other correlates with the length of the EVS. Buswell's

findings were accepted and reported by O'Brien (1926)—
"The width of the eye-voice span shows little correlation
with position in the line, except that the span at the end of a
line is slightly narrower" (p. 74)—and by Vernon (1931) and
Tinker (1965).

Fairbanks (1937) treated the position in the *line* and the
position in the *sentence* similarly. These are two very different phenomena. Line position is a mechanical issue, and
sentence position concerns constraints within and across
sentence boundaries, hence involving grammatical structure
and meaning. Separations between voice and eye are
greatest at the beginning of the line. However, the first fixation in a line is usually too long for both good and poor
readers, so a refixation follows. "The eye-voice lead at
refixations is probably a better measure of the lead at beginnings of lines, and has been seen to approximate the mean
for all pauses" (p. 84). Likewise, Fairbanks reports that the
mean at the ends of lines is nearly equal to the mean for all
pauses. In fact, the mean EVS at the ends of lines is so
close to the overall average EVS length that it can safely be
used as one diagnostic measure.

To sum up, the EVS does not appear to change as a function of position in the line. The spans in sentences may be
better postponed to the discussion of grammar and meaning.

Typography

Levin and Jones (1968) altered the typographic nature of the
text primarily to make it more difficult for readers to use
grammatical structure in their reading. It is useful, however,
to see how adulteration of the physical form of texts influenced the EVSs. The texts were 32 paragraphs selected from

those used by Levin and Kaplan (1968). In 16 paragraphs each interword space was filled by the letter X. Variations in this study concerning grammatical structure of the sentences, phrase length, and light-out position will be discussed in chapter 8. The notion was that the elimination of spaces between words would hamper the readers' scanning and force them to a word-by-word identification of the text, characteristic of younger readers. The subjects in this study were college students. The mean EVS for the X condition was 1.72 words; for normal text, 4.36 words. The difference is statistically significant (p < .001).

Another explanation of their findings is that the small EVS is not due to the obliteration of interword spaces but to the fact that since X shares graphic features with other letters of the alphabet, the readers were misinformed about the beginnings and ends of words. A second group of 8 adult readers participated in a set of conditions where interword spaces filled by asterisks (*) and X's were compared. Under both conditions, the sizes of the EVSs were equally small.

The conclusion appears reasonable that scanning ahead in the normal EVS situation is seriously affected by typographic abnormality, such as depriving the readers of spaces between words; the eye is then about two words in advance of the voice. Readers could possibly learn to react to consistent fillers as though they were spaces, but we doubt that the long experience with spaces between words can ever be totally overcome. Further, the deleterious effects of a variety of filler symbols interspersed with no particular order should be practically impossible to overcome.

The Levin and Jones study also removed interword spaces at selected points in the sentence to test hypotheses about the points in the grammar of the sentence that are likely to be deleterious to reading, that is, to the size of the EVS. These results are discussed in chapter 8.

In order to separate perceptual and syntactic factors that influence the EVS, Resnick (1970) had one group of college students read text that was projected upside down. The average EVS for this perceptual strain group was 2.75 words, compared to 4.67 words for college students reading standard text. The magnitude of this difference is similar to Levin's and Jones's results when the spaces between words were filled. Again, it appears that abnormal typography forces readers into a word-by-word strategy, which prevents them from using those constraints in the flow of text that facilitate reading.

Languages Other Than English
The grammatical and semantic constraints in different languages provide natural variations for the study of the EVS. German's multiply-embedded structures might yield confirmation of our findings regarding the EVS in right- and left-embedded sentences. Orthographic systems that provide the reader with different units of information would be interesting to study. For example, the same language written in two scripts—as Serbo-Croatian in Cyrillic and Roman script—might permit the isolation of the effects of writing systems per se. There have been various cross-language comparisons of reading achievement (Gray 1958; Thorndike 1973), but the EVS has been studied only with the English, Hebrew, and Japanese languages.

Schlesinger's (1968) results in Hebrew diverge from those in English in several important respects, but they agree in others. Morton (1964) and Lawson (1961) both reported that by decreasing the approximation to English, the size of the EVS decreased. These findings have been subsumed under the general principle that linguistic constraints, which are absent in low-order statistical approximations to the language, lead to large EVSs. Schlesinger's results do not agree. He used texts of second, fourth, and sixth order of approximation to Hebrew and found no significant differences in the EVSs of 18 university students. We may speculate that the differences between Lawson's and Morton's findings in English and Schlesinger's in Hebrew are due to the differences in the languages—a post hoc analysis that seems inevitable when the two languages are compared. In both sets of studies the EVS was measured as the number of *words* reported after the critical point. Hebrew words contain more morphemes than English and are also shorter, since the writing system omits vowels. These two factors may account for the incomparability of results.

In other respects, though, the Hebrew and English results are similar. For example, Schlesinger reports that the "last word in the EVS tends to be the last word in a chain" (p. 30). The span coincided with the end of a chain approximately seven out of ten times.

Schlesinger found that when readers reported the last word in a constituent incorrectly, the error functioned to make the span end at a constituent boundary. "We might speculate that the tendency to perceive a complete syntactical constituent may lead to a distortion in perception which is congruent with it" (p. 36). The English studies show the same kinds of configurations.

Fast readers of English, more often than their slower

counterparts, end their EVSs at constituent boundaries. Schlesinger had predicted that *slower* readers of Hebrew, with shorter spans, would read to phrase boundaries more often, because they could prepare their ends by looking ahead. The implication seems to be that rapid readers go through the text pell-mell, with little attention to structure: they would take in many words at once and not be able to control their spans. Schlesinger found that fast and slow readers terminated their EVSs at constituent boundaries with equal frequency.

Japanese has a unique writing system composed of Chinese characters (Konji) and two syllabaries (Kana). The usual writing system, as in newspapers, is a combination of Konji and Kana. In addition, there is a romanization used to teach Japanese to foreigners. Clarke (1972) used various forms of Japanese in her preliminary study of the EVS in reading Japanese. Besides the writing system differences, Japanese contrasts with English in structure; Japanese is not an Indo-European language. Finally, all EVS research has been done with horizontally written texts. Japanese is written vertically[1]

Eighteen native speakers of Japanese and seven native speakers of English, all advanced students of Japanese, were subjects in Clarke's research. Each was tested on three modes of Japanese writing: romanization, Kana syllabary, and normal Japanese, with Konji and Kana. Each subject read paragraphs and word lists in the three orthographies.

The clearest finding is that for all writing modes, the EVS is longer for connected sentences within a paragraph than for random word lists. In Japanese, as in other languages, the constraints formed by the language's structure enhance reading compared to unconnected forms. Also, whether the EVS is measured in words, syllables, or symbols, native speakers of Japanese have longer EVSs on the Konji-Kana form than on the Kana alone. Although it is tempting to explain this finding as being due to the Konji's functioning as units of both sound and meaning or marking word or phrase boundaries, the simplest explanation is that the native Japanese were most familiar with the Konji-Kana writing.

The findings from the Hebrew and Japanese studies are tantalizing. It would be exciting to have detailed information about the process of reading various languages and writing systems. Although not by design, English, Hebrew, and Japanese provide a wide sampling of writing systems— alphabetic, syllabic, and logographic—and direction—left to right, right to left, and top to bottom. Structurally and semantically they are Indo-European and non-Indo-European. Despite these differences, the findings at the most abstract level are similar. Readers of all languages exhibit EVSs when reading aloud, and the EVS is longer on connected prose, which has the constraints of grammar and meaning, than on lists of unrelated words.

5

CHARACTERISTICS
OF THE READER

Age

As we do so often, we call once again on Buswell (1921)
to give the reasons why, in the larger terms of knowledge
about the reading process, it is useful to know whether
readers as they grow older, and presumably more experienced, show longer EVSs.

A mature reader tends to maintain a comparatively wide average span between the eye and the voice, which at times
may amount to the space occupied by seven or eight words.
An immature reader, however, tends to keep the eye and
voice very close together, in many cases not moving the eye
from a word until the voice has pronounced it. Reading of
this type becomes little more than a series of spoken words
because there is no opportunity to anticipate the meaning in
large units. An eye-voice span of considerable width is
necessary in order that the reader may have an intelligent
grasp of the material read, and that he may read it with good
expression. If words are encountered which are spelled alike

but pronounced differently, such as "read" (present tense) and "read" (past tense), the correct pronunciation and meaning cannot be determined in many cases until the eye has observed the context by looking ahead. The need for a wide eye-voice span is also emphasized when marks of punctuation are encountered. The failure of immature readers to respond to a question mark by a rising inflection of the voice is clear evidence that a narrow eye-voice span has kept them unaware of its presence until it is too late to modify their expression. (p. 217)

Since our basic thesis is that the EVS reflects the reader's use of grammar and meaning in the text, the developmental course will indicate the reader's ability to use these higher-order characteristics of the material.

Buswell's (1920) basic data on age changes in the EVS are summarized in figure 5.1. Since he studied only 4 students at each grade level (6 in the college classes), none of his data points is stable, unfortunately. Thus, the development of the EVS, though irregular, is definitely upward. At the college level the age changes of the EVS are not so evident as at the lower grades. The sharpest rise in the developmental curve of the EVS occurs during the second, third, and fourth grades. There is some gain for the high-school readers (15.2 letter spaces) compared to the average for the fifth, sixth, and seventh grades (14.9 letter spaces). The fourth grade seems to be critical.

Buswell's age findings are seconded by Anderson and Dearborn (1952) and by Tinker (1965). Levin and Turner (1968) studied 10 subjects at each of six age levels: second, fourth, sixth,[1] eighth, and tenth grades and adults. The elementary school children read prose written with second-grade vocabulary, the others with sixth-grade vocabulary.

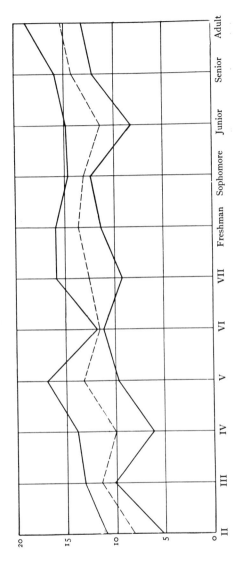

5.1
Development of EVS for good
readers (upper line), poor
readers (lower line) and all
readers (middle line) (Buswell
1920).

For all age levels the mean length of the EVS on unstructured word lists was shorter than on real sentences. So even at the second-grade level, context has an effect on the EVS. The EVS increased with age, although the eighth graders tended to read with longer spans than the tenth graders. Since the subjects volunteered from their study halls for "a reading experiment," there was no control for the ability of the readers obtained; this deviation is probably due to characteristics of the groups at both grade levels.

Levin and Cohn (1968) also found that the general tendency was for older subjects to have longer EVSs. Second graders had the shortest EVSs, and eleventh graders the longest. The fourth and ninth graders reverse the expected order. It should be pointed out that the second and fourth graders read second-grade materials and the two older grades read tenth-grade prose, which suggests that the lower-than-expected EVS scores for the ninth graders may have been due to the difficulty of their reading materials. This experiment was designed to test the effects of instructions on the size of the EVS. The results were consistent within each grade level: shortest EVSs when the instructions were to read carefully, longer to read "normally," and longest to skim. It is noteworthy that the effects, though not large, were evident as early as the second grade.

Using methods similar to Levin's, Resnick (1970) reported increasing EVSs for third graders, fifth graders, and college students, though only the youngest group differed significantly from the college students. Finally, Rode (1974–1975) and Zollinger (1974) found that the length of the spans increased from the third to the fifth grades. In all, the evidence is overwhelming that readers increase their EVSs as they grow older. There may be various reasons for this increase: perceptual spans increase with age; memory is better with age; and older readers are better able to use knowledge of grammar and meaning in reading, which leads to longer spans. The last explanation forms the basis for chapters 7 and 8, but a preview may be seen in the next section, which summarizes the evidence that older subjects report EVSs coinciding with the phrase structure of the text.

Age and Incidence of Reading to Phrase Boundaries
An important characteristic of EVSs is that they tend to end at phrase boundaries. This finding modified by information about the specific grammatical nature of the phrase probably has been the most important outcome of the research on the EVS. At what ages does this phenomenon become evident? In one study college students read to phrase boundaries more often than second graders, and the grade levels between these two extremes showed no increasing phrase-boundary effects (Levin and Turner 1968). Resnick (1970) did find an increasing incidence of stops at phrase boundaries for third graders, fifth graders, and college students, though she too reported that only the two groups most disparate in age were statistically significant.

Rode's (1974–1975) study was a more detailed and careful attempt to understand the relationship of age to phrase-boundary-EVS, and her results suggest reasons for the meager findings in the above two studies. Paradoxically, her third-grade pupils read to phrase boundaries more often than children in the fourth and fifth grades. Since her older readers had longer EVSs but did not stop at the phrase boundaries more often, what comprised the longer EVSs? Rode scored the number of times an EVS was equivalent to an entire clause—a unit containing more than one grammatical phrase. The two older groups read more often to clause boundaries. That is, they appeared to read in larger "chunks" equivalent to more complete units of meaning in the text. The above results were obtained by scoring only those EVSs that were reported without errors. Of the 392 miscues obtained in the study, 62 percent yielded syntactically and semantically correct prose. This characteristic of reading errors has been well documented by Weber (1970). When acceptable errors are included in the EVS score, the number of times the EVS extended to a clause boundary increased, and the magnitude of the increase was similar for all age groups. "This would seem to indicate that children at three levels of reading proficiency utilized already developed language skills to aid the decoding process and attempted to derive meaning from the text in units larger than the phrase" (p. 136). Rode believes that the three groups were all using syntax to the same degree, but that the third graders, who completed the most phrase units and the fewest clause units, were limited by their memory capabilities. The performance of the fourth and fifth graders was the same, so it seems that "by the fourth grade subjects tend to 'chunk' phrase units together" (p. 139) because they have longer memory spans. The fourth grade's performance is reminiscent of Buswell's (1920) finding that the size of the EVS rose sharply to the fourth grade and slowly in later grades.

Rate of Reading
When the eyes precede the voice in oral reading, the reader picks up a variety of information on how to intone, stress,

pause, etc. If the reader is operating at the limits of the speed at which he or she can articulate, the advance information can have little effect on the speed of oral reading. In most cases we assume that the reader is not coursing through the text lickety-split, so the reading rate may be influenced by basic reading skills, which include the use of word recognition, meaning, and structural information picked up by the eyes prior to the voice. In this section we ask whether long EVSs are associated with rapid rates of reading. We believe that longer forward sweeps of the eyes lead to more rapid oral reading rather than the reverse. It is difficult to make a reasonable argument that fast articulation "pushes" the eyes further ahead.

The methods of EVS studies are easily adapted to the investigation of rate. Whether the method involves the recording of eye movements or the memory for text beyond a light-off position, the investigator can time the oral reading at least to the light-out position and calculate a rate score, usually words or syllables per second.

Quantz (1897) hinted at the rate-span relationship, though his measure was of the speed of *silent* reading. "Those who are rapid silent readers read farthest ahead of the voice in reading aloud, and if a certain considerable distance between eye and voice is a condition of intelligent and intelligible reading, it follows that here again, as in silent reading, rapidity is an advantage" (p. 48).

Though Buswell (1920) found large variations in reading rate among elementary-school children, the relationship between rate and the EVS is marked. The reading rates of high-school compared to younger students are more uniform, between 2 and 4.9 words per second; again those with large

EVSs read faster. "The evidence here is perfectly clear that a wide EVS is a characteristic of rapid readers for subjects of all grades of advancement from the second grade of the elementary school to the college. . . . Rapid reading without a correspondingly wide EVS would be a monotonous or 'singsong' pronunciation of words" (p. 53).

In order to demonstrate that the intrinsic contextual constraints make it easier to read, Morton (1964b) had his adult subjects read statistical approximations to English, as well as a normal English passage. He believed that the increased probability of a stimulus made it easier to perceive; as the list of words came closer to English, the higher-order approximations and the real text would be read more rapidly and would yield longer EVSs. The subjects were instructed to read as fast as possible and not to try to give the passages meaning, since they were nonsense. The text also was to be read as fast as possible, without regard to punctuation or meaning. This is difficult to do. In our experience it is almost impossible for readers to pretend that meaningful prose is nonsense to be read with list intonation. The normal structure of the prose is so compelling that readers cannot overcome their tendencies to read with appropriate pauses, emphases, intonations, etc. The mean speed of reading in seconds per syllable increased to the fifth order, with little change between the fifth and eighth orders of approximation. People read the text more rapidly than any of the approximations, in spite of the fact that many subjects observed the punctuation and meaning pauses.

Morton divided his group into fast and slow readers. When the EVSs were measured in syllables or letter spaces, the spans increased up to the eighth order for both types of readers. Faster readers had larger spans, but the differences were not significant until the sixth order. In other words, both the rate of reading and the influence of the rate on the EVS occur only with materials that approximate normal text. Fast and slow readers behave similarly on random listlike materials. Morton's results demonstrate that the fast-slow distinction is really a measure of skill in using the constraints of meaning and grammar in reading.

That fast readers have longer EVSs holds as a generalization for a wide range of ages (Levin and Turner 1968). Subjects were classified as fast or slow readers on the basis of their reading rates up to the light-off position. Among second, fourth, sixth, eighth, and tenth graders and adults, faster readers in each group showed longer EVSs. In this study the reader's recognition as well as recall EVSs were measured. After recall—the usual procedure—subjects were shown a list containing five words that were actually present, three words beyond the critical light-out point and five distractors. Again, for all age levels the fast readers recognized more words correctly than their slower counterparts.

A major problem investigated in recent EVS studies is whether the span tends to end at a phrase boundary. These studies will be discussed in chapter 7. For our present purposes one may ask whether reading rate is related to the frequency with which subjects report EVSs that coincide with phrase boundaries. Fast readers more often reported their EVSs to conclude at phrase boundaries, which suggests that fast readers are more skilled at using the sentence's grammar to form reading units. Slower readers appear to read less maturely, that is, on a word-by-word basis.

Schlesinger (1968) selected two groups of subjects that he

termed ''fast'' and ''slow'' readers based on the average lengths of their EVSs. We infer, therefore, that among Hebrew readers he found the usual correlation between rate of reading and size of EVS. However, contrary to Levin and Turner, in two thirds of the cases both fast and slow readers reported EVSs with final words that coincided with the final word of a phrase.

Levin and Cohn (1968) demonstrated that the EVS is responsive to the intentions of the readers as determined by instructions to the subjects. Within each of the various grades—second, fourth, and ninth—and instructional conditions—to read normally or carefully or to skim—the correlations between reading rate and size of EVS were substantial. Again, fast readers had longer EVSs.

To sum up, there is strong evidence that rapid oral readers have longer EVSs, and it is probable that fast readers tend to end their spans at phrase boundaries, though this finding is not unequivocal.

Instructions to the Reader
Even the most casual introspection will indicate that mature readers vary their ''reading styles'' under a host of circumstances. We read differently, although we may not realize exactly how, when we are reading different types of material and when we are reading for different purposes. Casual perusal of the newspaper is different than reading to savor Wordsworth's style. Relaxing with an Agatha Christie thriller elicits reading far different than a text on symbolic logic. In fact a mark of a skilled reader is the facility to change reading behavior to suit the task.

There has been some research on the ways that textual

difficulty influences the EVS and eye movements during silent reading. These studies will be reviewed later. The reader's attitude, set, or intention have demonstrable and consistent effects on eye movements but rarely have been studied in relation to the EVS. However, since some of the eye-movement variables—length of forward shift of the eyes, number and duration of fixations, regressive eye movements, etc.—are involved in the EVS, the eye-movement experiments appear relevant.

C. T. Gray (1917) contended that although the duration of fixation pauses did not vary to any large degree, the number of pauses and regressive movements did change appreciably with the different types of reading his subjects were asked to do. They read in smaller units when they were to be questioned about the text than when they were asked only to reproduce the "general thought." An even clearer statement of similar results was made by Judd and Buswell (1922). They found that subjects who were instructed to read for detail tended to increase the number and decrease the duration of fixational pauses and to increase the number of regressions. The authors concluded that a mental set for close reading is answered by a procedure using smaller reading units, while longer units are employed for more superficial reading. Even greater differences occurred when the subjects were instructed to paraphrase the material; this reading set yielded even smaller units. Vernon (1931) claims that reading is most irregular (from the eye-movement data) when disturbed by conflicting interests or emotional tensions. Pressure to read quickly or to learn all the details from a single reading may produce irregular eye movements and confuse the reader.

Anderson (1937) compared the eye movements of good

and poor readers as they read silently under various instructions. The shortest fixation pauses of the good readers resulted from instructions to read for the general ideas, whereas poor readers demonstrated their shortest pauses under the normal condition: to obtain a moderate knowledge of the text. On all of the eye-movement measures, the instruction to read for the general idea yielded the largest differences between good and poor readers. The size of fixation decreased to almost the same figure for both ability groups under the detailed-reading instruction. The largest forward shifts were found under the general-idea-condition, followed by the moderate-knowledge-condition, and were smallest in the detailed-reading-condition, although *the effects of the instructions were consistently greater for the skilled than for the poor readers.*

The several eye-movement studies suggest that the EVS should be responsive to the intentions of the reader. Levin and Cohn (1968) carried out such a study with 60 public school students; 15 each from the second, fourth, ninth, and eleventh grades. The texts consisted of twenty-two short selections. The elementary-school children read selections classified as second-grade level; the upper two grades read tenth-grade passages. Each passage contained six sentences of meaningful, connected discourse. The critical sentence, in which the light was turned out, was either the third, fourth, or fifth sentence of the passage. An example of a critical sentence is:

The boys/followed their mother into the store.

(The slash indicates the light-out point.) The critical sentences were grammatically consistent; they began with a

noun phrase of either one, two, or three words, followed by
a three-word verb phrase, and a three-word prepositional
phrase. The higher-level selections concluded with an additional three-word phrase. The light-off position was always
between the subject and verb phrases and allowed sufficient
available words for the readers to exercise their full EVSs
on a single line: six words for the younger readers, and nine
for the older.

One practice selection under "normal" instructions was
given to each subject. The remaining twenty-one selections
were presented in groups of seven. Each group was introduced by instructions designed to create a set for *normal
reading,* especially *careful reading,* or *skimming* (par-
entheses denote changes for the older subjects):

1. Now, I'd like you to read me this story (passage) just the
way you normally would if you were reading out loud for the
teacher (or to a friend).

2. Now, this time, I want you to read me the story (passage)
very carefully. Pay close attention to all the details, because
I'm going to ask you questions about it afterwards. [One
question was asked after each of these passages.]

3. This time, you don't have to pay such close attention to
each (individual) little detail. Instead, I'd like you just to
read through for the general idea of the story.

The order of instructions was randomized for each subject.

The results are summarized in table 5.1. As hypothesized,
instructions to read carefully resulted in the shortest EVS
(3.69 words); normal reading was longer (3.97), and skimming was the longest (4.14). The same order of EVS size
was true for each of the four grades.

Table 5.1
Mean EVS (words) by instructions and grade
(Levin and Cohn 1968)

Instructions	Grade			
	2	4	9	11
Normal	2.95	4.32	3.97	4.64
Careful	2.92	4.04	3.73	4.09
Skimming	3.09	4.59	4.07	4.82

The effects of the instructions on reading rate are difficult to understand. Rate was calculated by the number of words per second read to the light-off position. Within each condition and grade the sizes of the EVS and reading rate showed strong and positive correlations, agreeing with the earlier general finding. However, in view of the fact that the EVS and rate normally go hand-in-hand, it is difficult to explain why the rates did *not* differ under the different instructional conditions. It appears that the instructions had no effect on the oral reading of the words in the passage and that the effects were confined to the movement of the eyes, "pushing" them further ahead of the spoken word. The limits on the rate of articulation may have been implicated in these findings.[2]

Comparing the scores for the normal condition with the average EVSs obtained under careful and skimming reading sets, it becomes apparent that in the early grades, the normal scores are very close to the careful ones, whereas, at the high-school level, the general idea (skimming) condition yields EVSs more similar to the normal. These findings suggest that normal reading for the beginners entails processes they customarily use for detailed reading; the reading is word-by-word, with close attention to each word and little forward scanning. In comparison, older readers ordinarily read for the general ideas, so this attitude is similar to the normal for them.

These conjectures fit well with Anderson's (1937) findings of the eye movements of good and poor readers. He cited the "inability" of poor readers to adopt any other than their everyday reading attitude, but he found that good readers, "on the other hand, showed their most regular eye-movement patterns in reading for the general ideas" (p. 18). In Anderson's good readers and the more mature readers of the current study, the elementary skills of reading are well developed. Therefore these subjects succeeded in adjusting their reading behavior to comply with the more subtle interpretations demanded by the material. Immature readers, highly engrossed in the elemental concerns, tend to read all materials in almost the same manner.

Reading Ability

Educational research that purports to compare good and poor students must be approached cautiously. The research problem may be the most common one in all research on schooling, yet the results are often contradictory and the findings elusive. The problems lie in determining which students are "good" and which "poor." Because these groups are identified by various criteria—tests, ratings, self-evaluations, observations of achievement—the studies are difficult to compare. Also, the criteria often capture heterogeneous groups, so trustworthy findings are rare in relation to the research energies invested. In spite of these pessimistic expectations the question, Do good readers have longer EVSs than poor readers?, can be answered with certainty. It can even be expanded to inquire whether good readers have more variable EVSs than their less able cohorts and to what the variability may be attributed.

Good and poor readers were usually identified by their scores on one or another reading test; sometimes they were categorized by the number of errors they made in reading. Speed of reading in a test or on the EVS task itself sometimes depends on reading ability.

Gray (1917) worked from eye-movement and EVS records (see ch. 2) to the reading abilities of the subjects. Initially, his group was unselected for reading ability. He gives examples of two "distinct types of eye-voice separation." In the first, the reader had a reasonably long span, three to four words, whereas the second reader's eyes and voice were close. Gray reported that the reader with the longer EVS was one of the best oral readers in his college-student group and that the second had not ranked so high. The major measure of oral reading ability was Gray's Oral Reading Paragraphs, from which four types of reading errors could be scored. The subjects were also graded on poise, pitch, articulation, pronunciation, emphasis, force and interpretation. Reading rate could be derived from the test, too. However, the composite scores that Gray reported did not clearly differentiate the two readers on ability, though their EVS patterns were indeed different.

Buswell (1920) thoroughly studied the EVS performance of 54 good and poor readers. On the basis of their scores on Gray's Oral Reading Paragraphs, two good and two poor readers were chosen from each of the elementary grades above the first. Based on the judgments of the English

Department and the school principal, three good and three poor readers were chosen from each of the four high-school classes. Six college students were chosen randomly, then divided into two ability groups. At the time of the experiment, the reading rates of all subjects were measured.

Buswell reported these findings: (1) in the elementary grades, there were large differences in the EVSs of good and poor readers; (2) the difference is also found, though to a lesser extent, in high-school students; and (3) among college students the differences were again large. Figure 5.1 shows Buswell's findings.

Buswell also found that good readers at all grade levels had *flexible* spans and that their EVSs varied with position in the sentence. Good readers had shorter spans at the ends of sentences—indications that they understood the meanings of the sentences and appreciated the conclusions of "thought units." Skilled readers also had longer spans at the beginnings of sentences; the initial wide span permits readers to grasp the nature of the material before they begin voicing. The initial span for the poor reader is no wider than the average.

For the poor reader, oral reading is evidently a monotonous process of passing over words without any great attempt to emphasize what is read. The good reader varies his span at different positions in the selection in order to bring about a better emphasis. . . . The study indicates, therefore, that for elementary-school pupils a variation in the width of the span for different positions is a characteristic of good reading more than of poor reading, and that for good readers the span is wider at the beginning of a sentence, a little narrower within a sentence and much narrower at the end of the sentence. . . . These data are very suggestive of a causal relationship between width of eye-voice span and the interpretation of meaning as exhibited by the treatment of a sentence as a unit of thought and the modification of the eye-voice span to fit such a unit. (Buswell 1920, p. 45)

Buswell, it will be recalled, worked with detailed eye-movement records of his subjects. There was no consistent relationship between the width of the EVS and the number of regressive eye movements per line. Readers of high and low ability differed, however, in the nature of their regressions. One type of regression was preceded by a short EVS and was characteristic of poor readers. Among good readers regressions were preceded by long EVSs. Buswell concluded that the former regression occurred when the reader was confused and unable to recognize words; the latter, when the reader had taken up an excessive amount of material and had to regress to grasp the meaning. Buswell refers to these as "sacrifices" made by good readers as they attempt to increase their EVSs.

Reading rate and reading skill are usually closely related. (There are no implications about speed reading in this statement.) Buswell found that at all age levels rapid reading was associated with wide EVSs. Investigators subsequent to Buswell, with a single exception discussed below, cited and confirmed his finding that skilled readers have wider EVSs. O'Brien (1926) averaged results from grades two through seven and reported that good readers have a span of 13.8 letter spaces compared to 8.7 letter spaces for less-skilled readers. The large span, he wrote, facilitates comprehension and more meaningful reading. Vernon (1931) offers a mechanical explanation for Buswell's results. Skilled readers assimilate (comprehend?) the text rapidly, but their rate of *articulation* is much slower. The *discrepancy* produces an interval between perception and vocalization, thus the EVS. She assumes what has been well demonstrated: that a good reader is also a rapid reader. A wide span is part of good oral reading, because it allows correct pronunciation, emphasis, and sentence rhythm.

Pedagogical practice for one decade before and at least one decade after Buswell's important monograph was guided by the belief that reading was a congeries of motor habits. Further, the Watsonian dictum held that all habits were trainable. The consequences were programs to teach effective eye movements and wide EVSs. Buswell's discussion of the causal relations between reading skill and EVS is reasonable. "The question was raised as to which of the two (good quality reading and a wide EVS) is cause or effect. It would appear that both are effects, and that the causal element is the existence of a general attention span wide enough to hold a large number of words or reading elements in the mind at one time" (p. 101). Thus, reading skill is a combination of higher-order skills, such as attention span and memory (see Gibson and Levin 1975), the consequences of which are efficient eye movements and appropriately wide and variable EVSs. Training for the consequences of reading skill is useless.

Fairbanks's (1937) is the one study whose results are difficult to reconcile with the consistent picture of substantial correlations between reading skills and size of the EVS. His good readers scored above the 90th percentile on the Iowa Silent Reading Test, and his poor readers, below the 10th percentile. Notice that he defined reading skill by a test of silent reading and then observed oral reading behavior. From our discussion in chapter 3 the assumption that good silent readers are good oral readers is not unreasonable, though it should be made cautiously. He reported that in general what he called the eye-voice lead was longer at all points for good readers. After more detailed analysis, Fairbanks claimed that at points of difficulty poor readers read more slowly and hesitated, thus increasing their EVSs so that they were wider than those of good readers. What seems to have happened is that the readers slowed their reading aloud without moving their eyes to the point of difficulty in the text. Further, at the site of oral reading errors, good readers reduced their EVSs to 2.29 percent of a line; poor readers showed less contraction, only reducing their spans to 7.41 percent of a line. "Regressions of this type reduce the lead practically to zero in good reading while in poor reading the amount is not strikingly lower than the average lead at all regressions. . . Good readers apparently are able to regress almost exactly to the point of the voice when an error is made, without hesitation. The eye-voice lead of poor readers apparently is lengthened because of the need for hesitation" (p. 101).

One may speculate about the wide span for poor readers. Less-skilled readers may not recognize an oral reading error or may take longer to realize that they have made an error. Also, since they were selected for silent reading achievement, they may use the silent reading strategy of trying to disambiguate a difficulty by reading ahead. Skilled readers, in other words, may bring into play different skills for oral than for silent reading. Poor readers may not have such flexible strategies.

Geyer's (1966) findings appear to confirm this interpretation. His research concerns the temporal EVS; he believes that a constant time between the voice and eyes is necessary for smooth oral reading. For smooth reading to be possible, the input-output systems in reading must be balanced. To reach a balanced state, the systems would have to work at a rate determined by the slowest of the systems. For oral reading this would be the "contribution of subsystems producing the oral response. By reading orally, therefore, the reader would need to slow down his eye movements in order to maintain a balance with slower oral response" (p. 95). Not slowing down the eyes leads to stumbling oral reading, for example, regressions of the eyes to regain the lost material. The principal problem, Geyer feels, is maintaining a rate of eye movements appropriate for silent reading while reading aloud. *This disjunction he finds to be true of poor readers.*

Anderson and Dearborn (1952), Woodworth and Schlosberg (1954), and Tinker (1965) base their discussions on Buswell's findings. Good readers have longer EVSs, because they have wider attention spans that allow them to grasp a large number of elements at once. Good readers are also more aware of sentence or thought units and are more able to vary their EVSs by sentence position.

Smith (1971) reports that a skilled reader usually keeps his eyes four to five words ahead of his voice in order to keep his short-term-memory storage full. Smith also relates the more recent findings on phrase-boundary effects to reading skill. A good reader's EVS is not a constant four to five words; rather, it expands and contracts with the size of the phrase units.

Anderson's (1937) findings on the eye movements of good and poor readers parallel, and may underlie, the EVS results.

Good readers are able to adjust the size of their fixations to the difficulty of the material. They are also more flexible in their eye movements when reading for different purposes. Though both skilled and unskilled readers showed flexibility in their eye movements in response to different instructions, the good readers did so more effectively. Generally, the good readers had longer forward shifts than poor readers. Each of these findings for silent reading has a counterpart for oral reading and for the EVS. The longer forward shifts are similar to wider EVSs for good readers, and the flexibility findings correspond to the expanding and shrinking EVS depending on the nature of the text.

In summary, good readers have longer EVSs than poor readers and are able to vary their EVS according to the nature of the materials and the purposes of reading. Although the EVS is a consequence of higher cognitive skills, the relationships between reading ability and the EVS are consistent and robust enough to use the EVS as a measure of reading skill.

6

**TELEGRAPHY,
TYPEWRITING,
AND
MUSIC**

In a broad sense, the EVS may be thought of as occurring in
a task in which the same information is being treated simultaneously in two ways—by the eyes and the voice. Woodworth (1938) pointed out that there are two skills besides
reading that permit the consideration of the same information by two modalities with the possibility of a lag or span
between them: telegraphy and typewriting.

Telegraphy
Bryan and Harter (1897, 1899) carried out the classic research on the acquisition and performance of the skills of
telegraphy, which have strong similarities to the EVS in reading. The incoming auditory message—the clicks, dots, and
dashes—runs in advance of its transcription. "Copying behind" allows the operator to form higher-order units, such as
letters, words, and phrases, from the clicks and to punctuate
and capitalize appropriately. Bryan and Harter based their

studies on the introspections of a small number of skilled telegraph operators. Still, the findings fit well with more detailed and controlled studies of spans.

The novice telegrapher attends first to letters and even to the clicks making up the letter. The ear-hand span is practically zero. Next, when receiving, the operator attends to words and later to phrases and short sentences. With increasing skill the operator extracts more and more complex units from the flow of sound. The experts report that they do all of this automatically, without necessarily attending to the meaning of the message being received. This "mechanical" reception is not unlike that of typists who can expertly transcribe without being able to recall the message or of readers who can vocalize adequately with no attention to meaning. Perhaps it is more accurate to say "minimal attention to meaning," because operators report that even when transcribing automatically they detect errors and inappropriate words.

The structures of letter sequences within words and sequences of words within phrases play important roles in the distance behind the ear that the hand can copy. It is much easier to receive letters forming words than random letters, and words in connected discourse are more easily transcribed than disconnected words. Operators were asked what happened when they received disconnected words or a strange code or a list of numbers. One telegrapher reported that he could keep six figures in mind if they were in groups of three and separated by a comma; he could not remember three or four isolated figures.

The expert operator can copy behind six to twelve words. Bryan and Harter calculate this span to involve an average

of 237.7 clicks. Although that feat is impressive, it is misleading to think in terms of clicks, letters, and words, since
the skilled operator continually extracts from the simple
units much smaller numbers of higher-order units, depending
on the constraints inherent in the messages. It is interesting
to notice, in passing, how many of the observations underlying modern cognitive psychology were gathered and interpreted reasonably by Bryan and Harter before the turn of
the century.

Typewriting

Soon after the studies of telegraphy, Book (1908) reported
observations on the eye-hand or eye-finger span in typewriting. Like readers, typists read the text in advance of their
fingers striking the keys. With practice the typist advances
from attending to letters and syllables to attending to groups
of words, perhaps up to five. "When word associations were
sufficiently developed for the movements in certain connections to be made faster than the letters could be focussed individually by the eye, the copy had to be gotten further
ahead and the succession of movements controlled in some
other way" (Book 1908, p. 38). "Attention was pushed
ahead of the hands as far as possible (usually four or five
words), a sort of backward regard being maintained for the
general direction of the actual finger movements. . . The
advantage of thus getting the copy several words ahead of
the hands is that special attention can be given to any difficulties which may arise, for all the words and letters are
not equally easy even for an expert" (p. 44). Book believed
that the eye-hand span varied with the difficulty of the material, but the span never reduced to zero. Spelling out, when

necessary, was done ahead of the fingers, thus allowing continuous typing.

The development of the span for typewriting seems to be similar to that for telegraphy and for reading. Book mentions in passing that the expert typists' units of attention are phrases and clauses.

The joy of finding congruent evidence from reading, telegraphy, and typewriting is dispelled by Butsch's (1932) research. His basic apparatus and research design were modeled after Gray's. Records of the typists' eye movements and typewriting were taken simultaneously. However, since there is a strong tendency to move one's head while typing, Butsch used a very restrictive method of head fixation that included a bite board into which the typist's teeth were fitted. This restraint may help explain Butsch's findings. For every ten typewritten spaces, a mark was made on the eye-movement record so that the position of the eyes and the typewritten record could be coordinated.

Slower typists had shorter spans and more fixations; faster typists more often carry their spans over the ends of lines. The nature of eye movements during typing is very different from reading. There are many more fixations per line: the smallest number was 15.3 in a line of 60 spaces compared to Buswell's finding of 5.9 fixations per line during silent reading and 8.4 during oral reading. The fixations were also longer: "Apparently during typewriting the eye does not read at all at its maximum pace or even at the rate which is determined by the requirements of comprehension, but instead reads only rapidly enough to supply the copy to the hand as it is needed" (p. 111). With an increase in speed of typing, there was an increase in span as measured in spaces, though the temporal span was about one second, regardless of typing speed.

Butsch carefully analyzed the performance of one expert typist on various kinds of materials. On disconnected material—strings of words—the typist often took in groups of words. "This throws some doubt on the theory that the writing is done by phrases. An equally plausible explanation is that the eye simply moves ahead occasionally and takes in a longer span, irrespective of thought content" (p. 120).

We can only guess about why Butsch's findings differ from many other studies. Typists, in our experience, often report that they do not understand the materials they are typing and do not remember it after they are done. Typing can be a mechanical input-output task as can reading aloud. However, typists can try to understand the text, in which case the results would be more akin to the EVS during reading. Further, the artificiality and awkwardness of the head restraint in Butsch's research may have provided his typists with inadvertent instructions to focus straight-ahead and narrowly. In the end, we must accept these results as deviant and curious.

Hershman and Hillix's (1965) experimental methods were interesting variants of the usual "span" studies. The span, eye, ear, or hand, is usually the dependent variable, related to skill, nature of the text, etc. These investigators exposed varying amounts of text to the typists so that the size of the viewing aperture controlled the available span and functioned as an independent manipulation. They presented the same text in three versions: normal, connected text; random words; and random letters. The common text assured that the same typewriting skills were called for. There were five levels of exposure in the aperture: one, two, three, or six characters in the window or the entire selection. As a typewriter key was depressed, one character moved out of the window, and one was added.

The mean number of errors was 12.1 for the random letters, 6.6 for random words, and 6.7 for text. The mean errors for a single-character exposure was 12.7; for two, 7.2; for three, 6.7; for six, 8.8; and for unlimited, 6.7. The exposure variation produced the larger effect. There is most improvement as one moves from either words or connected text with the characters exposed one-by-one to an unlimited exposure.

Unlike reading, where the ability to form increasingly higher-order units improves performance, in typing the interdependent constraints among letters in words are as useful as larger units of connected text. The investigators believe that typists use preorganized responses that can be operative with exposures of at least three letters. "If a human observer is entering information from a display, the amount of information on the display should be sufficient so that the observer can use his paralleling capacities. Three random letters will let him use much of his capacity and six characters will allow him to enter words or text in a high percentage of his maximum efficiency" (p. 491). Hershman and Hillix's findings echo Butsch's that in typing the eye moves ahead almost irrespective of syntax or meaning to supply the hands with material.

Random words are more efficient to the typist than random letters, though not much more effective than connected text. The typist strikes the keys letter-by-letter but can hold words in memory because of the within-word constraints on

letters. Said another way, words form single units of a
higher order than letters; thus, words can be identified and
held in memory more efficiently than letters, since experienced typists can strike the keys at a faster rate than they
can read individual letters. "Since the response requirement
in typing is a letter by letter transliteration of text, the reading operation must partition the text into segments that can
be decomposed into letter strings with some acceptably low
risk of error through memory failure. It would thus be misleading to say that people can read faster than they can
type" (Schaffer and Hardwick 1969, p. 383). These researchers also imply that there is little comprehension in typing.

Although superficially similar, there are important differences among the EVS in reading, the ear-hand span in telegraphy, and the eye-hand span in typewriting. Woodworth
(1938) pointed out that the ear-hand span in copying a telegraphic message is especially long if one counts the number
of clicks in a message. Counting clicks is misleading, though,
since even with the most rudimentary telegraphy skills,
clicks are combined into higher-order units of letters, letters
into words, words into phrases, etc.

In typing, however, the span is only five or six letters,
enough to keep feeding material to the typist so that the typing proceeds continuously. Both of the spans are spatially
shorter than the EVS. However, the time spans for all three
are roughly the same—about one second. The motor requirements in each task are the principal reason for the differences. The motor acts in typing and telegraphy are slower
than vocalization, so the eyes must "put in the time some-
how" (Woodworth, p. 734). Telegraphy and typing are to
a great extent motor skills, so the spans increase with

improvements in those skills. By comparison, one is unlikely to say that the EVS increases with the ability to vocalize.

The EVS and the ear-hand span are influenced by phrase structure; the eye-hand span is not. Readers and telegraphers profit from understanding the material; use of the inherent structure simplifies the task. Oral readers need advance information to properly intone the text, and telegraphers must divide the message into sentences and punctuate and capitalize appropriately. Typists have no such task demands; the copy contains all of the information to be transcribed. The typist is a "pass through" who does not need to understand the copy.

Music
Reading music, playing an instrument, or singing have obvious similarities to reading text aloud. The span between the point of the eye's position on the musical notation and the point of performance on a musical instrument has been called the "eye-performance span" by Jacobsen (1941), that is, the distance that the eyes precede the performance. He recorded the eye movements of immature, average, and mature musicians. The least competent reader had a span of only one note and made a large number of fixations—some of very long duration—many regressions, and errors. The average music reader had a span of about two notes and had less than half as many fixations, shorter pauses, and a third as many errors as the immature reader. The immature reader had no obvious pattern of eye movements, whereas the average reader showed some regularity. Mature readers of music had fewer pauses and regressions than the other two, shorter pauses, and few errors.

These findings are similar to those for reading text. Eye movements and spans vary with the difficulty of the music. Jacobsen compared the reading of scale runs with arpeggios and found that all readers had longer spans and showed more regular eye movements on the former. These findings were true as well for other difficult aspects of music such as number of parts and whether the parts were bass or treble. Jacobsen's results were similar for vocal and instrumental music. He mentions the effects of the intrinsic structure of music only indirectly. Experienced musicians can "hear" the music when they look at a score, so the auditory replica provides a basis for a wider performance span.

Sloboda (1974a, 1974b, 1977), on the other hand, has investigated the reading of music in ways directly analogous to the study of the EVS; he was, in fact, influenced by the research on the EVS. Sloboda used the method of turning off the lights at predetermined positions in the music score and recording how much farther the subject played. Two groups were formed on the basis of ability—the number of errors they made to the light-off position. He reported a correlation of 0.89 between the subject's ability and the length of the eye-hand span. The best reader had a span of 6.8 notes; the worst, 3.8 notes. An important finding was that good readers read to phrase boundaries 72 percent of the time, whereas poor readers stopped at phrase boundaries only 20 percent of the time.

The phrase-boundary finding entailed the difficult problem of defining phrase boundaries in the musical score, essentially writing the grammar of the musical selection. Sloboda (1974a) believes that there are rules of well-formedness in music as in language. "It is possible, therefore, that good sight-readers have internalized the constraints and structures implicit in the music of their culture, and may use these to modify their reading behavior in a manner analogous to ordinary reading" (p. 2). Several judges independently determined the phrase boundaries of the musical texts. Critical, light-out, positions were selected with reference to the phrase structure. Correcting for the number of phrase-ending spans that would be predicted to fall on the phrase ending from the average span itself, Sloboda was able to demonstrate clearly that the eye-hand span tended to extend to the phrase boundary in the music. The result obtains with those subjects who performed with no errors; if the cases with one error are included, the number of times a span ended at a phrase boundary was even greater.

Sloboda explains these results by a "sophisticated guessing" theory. "This holds that expectancy, or response bias, will decrease the amount of sensory information required to precipitate an identification" (p. 9). Of the 181 errors, 90 were acceptable alternatives under very strict criteria, similar to the findings in reading.

In a later study Sloboda (1977) took apart the effects of physical compared to structural markers on the eye-hand span for keyboard musicians. Physical markers are the spaces to the right of notes that signal the time duration of the notes. Structural markers "arise primarily out of rules for harmonic progression which serve as 'grammatical' rules for music" (p. 118). The score was removed at predetermined points in the musical phrase. The eye-hand span ended at phrase boundaries when there were both harmonic phrase markers and physical phrase boundaries, but the influence of musical structure was substantially greater than physical boundaries.

Although spans in reading prose, telegraphy, typewriting, and reading music appear superficially similar, they are in fact alike in complex ways. Readers of prose and music and telegraphers take advantage of the structure in their materials to perform their tasks more economically and efficiently by extracting and using higher-order units. Typists, on the other hand, at least in the experimental settings, use the orthographic constraints within words but otherwise keep about one second ahead of their fingers; typists are not particularly influenced, except at the elementary level, by the structure of the materials they are copying.

7

GRAMMAR, MEANING, AND THE EVS

In this chapter and the next we turn from the EVS as such to the EVS as an index to the nature of the reading process. EVS research evolved from interest in the span's relationship to age, reading skills, physical characteristics of the text, etc.; partly because of the way it was measured, the study of the EVS and the study of eye movements grew up together. With the substantial background knowledge we now have about EVSs, we can use the span as a gauge to the nature of reading. The specific focus of our concern is how various kinds of text are read. The modern interest reflects our increased sophistication in describing English texts, a consequence of the psychologists' union with linguists.

The earliest researchers on the EVS strongly hinted that the span had something to do with meanings expressed in the texts. "Meaning units" were metaphors for intuitions that readers were not performing mechanically but were

influenced by the form of the textual information. We will
first review the early researchers' forays into grammar,
meaning, difficulty, and readability of the text. Since we will
try to make these intuitions clearer and amenable to direct
study by invoking English grammar, we describe how we think
grammar works to facilitate reading. We then ask, What
do we know about EVSs and the readers' eye movements
on which they depend that will provide a reasonable bridge
between grammatical structure and the EVS? We consider
the relationship between the EVS and grammatical units from
the general to the specific: no or little grammatical cohesion
in the text, sentences, and phrases. In the next chapter we
continue the discussion as far as we now can: to describe
types of phrases and clauses in various kinds of sentences.

Early Research on Grammar and Meaning
From the earliest experimental research on reading, one can
infer that the researchers recognized the relationships between the meanings in texts and the way they were read, or,
prescriptively, the ways they should be read. S. H. Clark
(1901, orig. 1898), without explicitly describing the EVS,
said that the reader must look ahead while reading and "so
rid himself of the too general tendency to utter words as
soon as he sees them, regardless of the sense" (p. 129). "If
the student were to vocalize as many words as he could see
and say as he saw them, his reading would be meaningless
and choppy. *Thought or sense should determine the places
to stop* [our emphasis]. The thought, and not the grammatical construction, determines the pause" (p. 130). "Every group
of words has a picture in it, and . . . we must not read
aloud any word until we have got the thought or the picture

in the group'' (p. 113). Clark, of course, was using an imagery theory of meaning characteristic of his time but saw clearly that meaning influences, or should influence, the way one reads.

Huey (1908) briefly pointed out that we can perceive more text when the items are combined in some sensible way, a finding that was available since Cattell's (1889) classic experiments on the recognition of letters, words, and sentences. Huey also implied that the function of the EVS is to allow the reader to understand what he is reading. "It is doubtless true that without something of this there could be no comprehension of speech at all" (p. 148). We have had many occasions to state Gray's (1917) and Buswell's (1920) belief that the span allowed the reader to grasp the content of the matter before voicing it.

Buswell (1920), following an idea of Quantz's, performed an ingenious experiment to demonstrate that the EVS is essential for understanding the text. Homographs are words that are spelled alike but pronounced differently and have different meanings depending on the surrounding text. For example, a reader would not know which pronunciation or meaning to give to *present* unless he knew whether the meaning intended was "to give" or "a gift." Levin, Ford, and Beckwith (1968) showed that the choice of alternative pronunciations of homographs is facilitated by textual information, which gives the homograph's part of speech.

Buswell's experimental paragraph is interesting enough to merit close inspection:

The boys' arrows were nearly gone so they sat down on the grass and stopped hunting. Over at the edge of the woods they saw Henry making a bow to a little girl who was coming down the road. She had tears in her dress and also tears in her eyes. She gave Henry a note which he brought over to the group of young hunters. Read to the boys it caused great excitement. After a minute but rapid examination of their weapons they ran down the valley. Does were standing at the edge of the lake making an excellent target.

The word "tears," for example, is ambiguous until the reader sees the word "dress," and later, "eyes." The expectation was that readers with long EVSs would make fewer errors in reading the homographs aloud, because they would have seen more words ahead of their voices and so would be able to disambiguate the homograph before pronouncing it.

People who read this paragraph both silently and aloud showed certain characteristic confusions in eye movements at the points of difficulty in the text. Readers with long EVSs made fewer errors in reading the homographs. Thus, a long EVS permitted the reader to take in enough information to understand and pronounce the critical words correctly.

Studies that related the span (and more frequently, the pattern of eye movements) to the difficulty of the text opened another avenue to understanding the connections between the meaning of the text and the EVS. Definitions of difficulty are not obvious. Buswell considered the presence of homographs as making the text more difficult to read and, by implication, to understand; in another study he introduced difficult—long, rare, specialized—words. A text may be difficult because of the manner in which the material is written, that is, a source of difficulty of understanding attributable to the text rather than the reader. Such determinations come under the rubric of *readability,* a long, difficult, and often confused area of study, thankfully beyond the compass of this book. On the basis of readability calculations, texts are described as appropriate for one or another grade level. Reading materials may be difficult to understand because of the reader's unfamiliarity with the words, the grammatical constructions, or the subject matter. Unfortunately, there is little EVS or eye-movement research based on careful analyses of the reasons for the difficulty of the text.

Buswell (1920) found short EVSs and long fixations associated with difficult words. The span is further reduced by regressions and rereading the unfamiliar words. Vernon (1931) used foreign reading material as difficult prose and obtained results that appeared to be the same as those of studies on reading incomprehensible prose in one's native language or reading native prose when the instructions were to read for details. Good readers are able to adjust the distance between fixations in response to the difficulty of the prose; poor readers are not (Anderson 1937).

Anderson and Dearborn (1952) provide an efficient summary of text readability and the size of the EVS:
The principal source of the intra-passage variation in the size of the EVS concerns the readability of the material itself. The span is at its widest when the material reads smoothly. It is reduced in size by the presence of difficult or ambiguous words and by the appearance of other sources of uncertainty and confusion. The eye *hesitates* [our emphasis] until the meaning is clear, which gives the voice a chance to *catch up with the eyes* [our emphasis]. Regressions operate to reduce the separation between the eyes and the voice. . . . Good readers have a wider and more elastic span than poor readers. (pp. 124–125)

Others (Woodworth and Schlosberg (1954) and Tinker
(1965), who has done the most extensive and careful modern
research on eye movements, reached the same conclusions:
difficulty, whether due to the nature of the text or to characteristics of the reader, reduces the size of the EVS. "But
when the reader meets a difficult word or concept, the span
becomes narrower. There is hesitation while the reader cogi-
tates, trying to clarify the meaning. . . This brief period of
hesitation allows the voice to catch up with the eyes. The
resulting variation in width of span characterizes the skillful
oral reader" (Tinker 1965, p. 86).

To sum up, the early researchers on the EVS often wrote,
but in a general way, about the influence of grammar and
meaning on the size of the span. Meaning was studied indirectly by arranging characteristics of the text that were
difficult to understand (homographs, difficult words, etc.);
the size of the EVS shrank at these points. Correct pronunciation was facilitated by long EVSs, which presumably
permitted the reader an advance view of the context that
disambiguated the homograph.

How Does Grammar Work?
Grammar is a set of rules that organizes morphemes and
words into acceptable sentences of a language (Chomsky
1965). As such, grammar provides a complex set of invariant
relations within language the reader uses. Written language
may be analyzed into various levels: letters, letter clusters,
syllables, morphemes, words, phrases, sentences, and discourse. A skilled reader takes advantage of the rules at the
various levels, often in parallel. Grammar is an intermediate
level, encompassing the lower-level invariants. As such,

grammar provides the *context* for the subsidiary units. There is massive evidence that context *narrows the alternatives* among the lower-order units. Grammatical rules supply the context that increases the efficiency of reading the subordinate units that these rules govern. The efficiency is realized by less attention to the subsidiary units, which implies that reading involves fewer fixations, briefer fixation pauses, and fewer regressions. Morton (1964b) puts it well: "In other words, the presence of context reduces the number of visual cues necessary for the correct identification of the words" (p. 176).

Context is efficient only if it is relevant to the identification of a word; grammar is relevant for the identification of words that form the grammatical structure in question. Besides the relevance of the context, its length is also important, and the amount of context and its relevance contribute independently to word identification (Tulving and Gold 1963). As we have noted earlier, increasing length of context narrows the range of alternatives (Aborn, Rubenstein, and Sterling 1959) so that ends of sentences provide more context than beginnings (Kolers 1970).

One could go on documenting the point that grammatical structure provides the context for facilitating a variety of reading-related behaviors. As mentioned before, Levin, Ford, and Beckwith (1968) gave high school students the task of choosing the correct pronunciation for homographically spelled words, such as *sow*-/so/ or /sau/, *present*-/ présent/ or présént/. The pronunciation depends on the context of the homograph. The latency for reading the homograph was determined when it was preceded by a synonym or by a grammatical cue as to its part of speech. Slides each containing one word, context or target, were presented in sequential pairs. One pair might be *pig-sow*, another, *to-sow*. The homograph was pronounced more rapidly when the preceding contextual word signaled its part of speech rather than its meaning. In both cases the pronunciation was more rapid than when there was *no* relevant context. These results are best interpreted to mean that a normal two-word phrase yields more rapid pronunciations than when the context supplies meaning but is not in the form in which it is usually spoken. The high school students found it easier to say the phrase "to present" than the word sequence "gift present."

In summary, our view of the many relationships between grammatical structure and reading is that *grammar provides the context that increases the economy of processing the units making up the grammatical structure.* How does this general hypothesis influence research on the EVS?

The EVS and Eye Movements

The most general and most important thesis of this and the next chapter is that *the EVS is responsive to the nature of the constraints (predictability, information) in the text. EVSs are longest at those points in the text that are the most constrained, that is, the most predictable, and that yield the least information.* [1] There are, therefore, certain implications for the pattern of eye movements depending on the constraints in the text that underlie the observed EVS: the eyes should make long saccadic jumps; there should be fewer fixations, which should be of short duration, and there should be fewer regressive eye movements. What is the evidence?

The empirical studies of eye movements and the size of

the EVS offer strong confirmation for these speculations. As
the EVS increased in length, the number of fixations decreased (Buswell 1920). In his research, the median duration
of fixations varied in the narrow range of 9/50 to 13/50 seconds, but there were some fixations that lasted up to 93/50
seconds. Buswell first hypothesized that the eye often got
too far ahead of the voice and paused to allow the voice to
catch up. When he inspected his eye-movement records in
detail, he found that after very long spans the eyes often
made a series of short fixations of brief duration. Then Buswell tested the hypothesis that fixations would be longer on
difficult words. One of his test passages contained the words
"hypnogogic," "hallucinations," and "hyperaesthesia."
High-school and college students fixated these words for abnormally long times, and other long fixations occurred in
places where the words or constructions were unfamiliar.
  Geyer (1966) has argued that one understands the EVS as
a period of time—a constant, temporal interval—determined
by the length of time that information can be held in short-
term memory. That is, the textual material between the eye
and voice is put into short-term memory, and smooth oral
reading requires an optimal time interval between the eyes
and voice. The eyes cannot be any farther ahead of the voice
than the amount of time that information can be held in short-
term memory. The eyes (the input system) will stop briefly
to resolve problems in the text at the same time as the voice
(the output system) continues, so that by the time the response system reaches the same point of difficulty, the input
system will have resolved the problem and reestablished the
previous lead. In other words, textual difficulties will involve
longer fixations succeeded by longer-than-usual forward

movements. At the points at which the balance between input and output was upset, such as beginnings and ends of sentences, Geyer found greater numbers of refixations and regressions, interpreted as means to "rebalance the system." Geyer later added that attempts to rebalance the system may also take the form of long fixations or short forward movements. Although cast in another nomenclature, this research also shows a relationship between the size of the EVS and certain kinds of eye movements.

Long EVSs are attended by long sweeps of the eyes and brief fixations at the point where the eyes come to rest. One would think, therefore, that regressive eye movements would show the opposite relationships to the EVSs. The results are far less clear. Regressive eye movements may show that the reader does not understand the text so that additional fixations are necessary. Buswell (1920) found no consistent relationships between the size of the EVS and the number of regressive movements per line. To understand this finding it is essential to separate the causes of the regressions. They happened when poor readers were confused and unable to recognize words or when skilled readers permitted their eyes to get too far ahead of their voices and the meaning of the passage was unclear, perhaps because the short-term memory store was overtaxed, as Geyer would say. Buswell studied all instances in his data where spans of nine or more letter spaces preceded a regression. This type of regression in eye movements, following a long EVS, was characteristic of skilled readers.

Most regressions follow an oral reading error (Fairbanks 1937). Good readers reduced their EVSs to 2.29 percent of a line after an error; poor readers maintained their modal EVS after an error, 7.41 percent of the line. "Good readers apparently were able to regress almost exactly to the point of the voice when an error is made, without hesitation. The eye-voice lead of poor readers apparently is lengthened because of the need for hesitation" (p. 101).

From the above research we may, with some certainty, accept our assumptions that long EVSs are constructed from long forward eye movements, fewer and shorter fixations. The role of regressions is a bit more complicated in that good readers respond to errors by regressions and shorter EVSs, and poor readers are less adaptive in their reading behavior.

For our purposes, we expect the constraints of grammar to result in longer EVSs, which are brought about by a pattern of eye movements that reflect the adequacy of less information for identifying grammatically constrained units.

No Structure and Statistical Approximations

If grammatical structure facilitates reading, the limiting cases are those texts that are simply unrelated lists of words, which by definition have no structure. In one study taking various ages together, the average EVS on grammatically normal text was 3.91 words; for word lists, the mean span was 2.19 words. These two means differ significantly (Levin and Turner 1968). Similarly, for a group of adults the average EVS for random word lists was about 2 words; there was little variation among readers (Levin and Kaplan 1968). The results are similar for Japanese (Clark 1972). Therefore, EVSs are predictably short when there is no structure in the text.

Miller (1963) wrote, "The eye-voice span should be slowest

where the information per symbol is greatest. . . . a fifth-order approximation to the statistical structure of English word sequences should read quite naturally" (p. 191). When the contributors to approximations to English are given a topic, the fifth-order sample reads like this (Miller, p. 192):

the umpire quickly shouted that Durocher had made his men work to perfect their skill at fielding is very good when the team isn't in the line-up today is one of the greatest players stood amazed at the plate while the batter swung at the pitch.

Miller's hypothesis was tested by Morton (1964a) who found that EVSs increased to the fifth or sixth approximation depending on the reader's skill and then showed no increase to the eighth approximation or to normal text. It should be noted that zero approximation is the same as a random word list. Lawson (1961) reported similar results. Schlesinger (1968) could not replicate these findings in Hebrew, which he attributes to the morphemic structure of Hebrew and to the omission of vowels in the orthography.

To sum up, in the comparison of structure versus no structure, the EVS is substantially longer on the former. When structure is defined in statistical terms, in English at least, the EVS is longer as the text is more similar to normal prose.

Sentences

The length of the EVS in the line of type is not really an important issue; the span within sentences, on the other hand, is important. Sentences have grammatical structure and represent a "unit" of meaning. We assume that the constraints within sentences usually are greater than those between sentences. This very general statement will be modified in chapter 8 to account for the nature and position of the intrasentence constraints, depending on the specific grammatical makeup of the sentence. As a first approximation, though, we may assume the unitary nature of sentences and ask how constraints of sentences—any sentence—affect the EVS.

As usual, Buswell (1920) recognized the important research question:

> The fact that the EVS varies with the position in the sentence is of considerable significance. If the span varied only with the position within the line, as Quantz's study indicated, the determining factors would be governed by the printed form of the selection. The control of the span, in that case, would be a matter of the mechanics of book construction and would be independent of any teaching factor. But if the span varies with position in the sentence, it is evident that the content of meaning is recognized, and that the EVS is determined by thought units rather than by printed line units. Position in the line may be a minor factor . . . but the differences due to position in the sentence are much greater. (pp. 48, 50)

Buswell, it will be recalled, measured the EVSs of good and poor readers of various ages from the early elementary grades to college. The clearest finding was that proficient readers in the elementary grades demonstrated very short EVSs at the ends of sentences; poor readers in the lower grades did not. At the beginnings of sentences good readers showed a wider than average span. The average of all subjects' EVSs was 15.9 letter spaces at the beginning of the sentence, 13.4 in the middle, and 10.9 at the end. The differences were even more marked when Buswell took the averages only for the good readers: 18.7, 16.5, and 11.9 letter spaces, respectively. For the poor readers, the span at the beginning was greater than that at the end for all age groups; the span at the beginning was greater than that in the middle for all but the elementary readers.

These findings and Buswell's explanation are difficult to reconcile with our hypothesis that the most constrained parts of the text will yield the widest EVSs. He believed that the longer spans at the beginnings of sentences were necessary to give the reader a chance to grasp the content before voicing it. Poor readers at the elementary levels began to read as soon as the sentence appeared, without first scanning ahead. The shorter EVS in the final position allows the voice to catch up with the eye before a new thought is begun. The pause that comes with the period not only lets the eye get a head start again, but expresses vocally that a thought has ended, that is, the voice expresses a sentence-ending contour.

There are various research findings to support our assumption that the ends of sentences are more constrained than the beginnings. Increasing the length of context narrows the range of possible alternatives (Aborn, Rubenstein, and Sterling 1959). Reading errors decrease over the final three-fifths of sentences (Kolers 1970), and there are more correct guesses in a cloze procedure at the ends of sentences (Miller and Coleman 1967).

If sentences are more constrained, in both structure and meaning, at their ends than at their beginnings, Buswell's findings are hard to understand. His results may be procedural and typographic artifacts. His readers were permitted

to look ahead before beginning to read. Many later
studies have been arranged so that the subjects begin to read
immediately with the onset of the visual text. Freedom to
scan the sentence before reading aloud is usually followed
by regressions of the eye, which implies that the distance between the eye and the voice is abnormally long. The vivid-
ness of the period truncates the EVS as much as does the
end of a line. Though Buswell's intention to interpret the
EVS as reflecting sentential meaning is exemplary, his results are explained by processes similar to the effects of the
typographic line.

Fairbanks's (1937) findings appear to confirm our explanations of Buswell's results. Fairbanks did find that the EVS
was shortest at the ends of sentences. He did *not* find the
span to be longer at the beginnings of sentences; rather, it
was nearly equal to the mean for all spans within the sentence. In his instructions Fairbanks stressed that a silent
reading situation was to be closely approximated: "The effect of the latter [an approximation to silent reading] is to increase the rate and cut down pause time, thus giving the eyes
less opportunity to increase their lead during pauses of
the voice" (p. 83). Fairbanks took his measure (both he and
Buswell had continuous eye-movement records) when the
eye (not the voice) was at the beginning of the sentence. At
this point the eye would not be too far ahead of the voice.
The quick increase in distance would not be expected until
the voice had at least reached the period of the preceding
sentence. Fairbanks did not even include this point in his
measurements. He measured when the eye was on the last
word in the sentence and the voice was further behind in the

same sentence. The second measurement was made when the eye fixated on the first word in the next sentence.

Fairbanks's explanation of the reduced span at the ends of sentences is that some difficulty is involved in ending one sentence and beginning another. At the end of a sentence the eye reduces its lead "in anticipation of a punctuation mark" (p. 84). Thus, Fairbanks's interpretation of EVSs within sentences agrees with ours, and his data support our explanation of Buswell's findings.

Vernon (1931) saw some merit in most of her predecessors'—Buswell, Quantz, Dearborn, etc.—findings, contradictory though they may seem. "The location and relative duration of the fixation pauses in the printed line are in part functions of fixed habits of movement, and tend to remain the same whatever the words in the line (i.e., are determined by line position); but they are also affected by the nature of the reading material (i.e., by syntactic/semantic aspects)" (p. 45). "Though, as a result of ocular motor habits, the fixation pauses may tend to occur predominantly in certain positions, yet their actual location is finally determined by the apperceptive units (read as 'grammatical and meaning') into which the text is divided" (p. 47). In support, she cites Dearborn's findings on the eye movements: "familiar words, or even phrases, required only a single fixation. . . . Any words which stood by themselves and could not be fused into a language unit, such as a phrase, demanded separate fixations" (Vernon, p. 46).

The early researchers on the EVS, and on eye movements, were aware that the structure of the text influenced the reading process, and they wrote about the phenomena frequently though imprecisely. Today, with a little poetic

license, we may read "apperceptive units," "meaning
units," "units that hang together," "thought units," etc., as
terminology of grammar and semantics. The results on the
sizes of EVSs at various points in sentences give little empirical support to the reasonable speculations. The sentence as
a unit is too gross to demonstrate the effects of the constraints of grammar, because unselected sentences may represent many forms of intrasentence constraints. Without
detailed analyses of the grammar of the experimental sentences, averages calculated on many types of sentences are
likely to show Fairbanks's results: the size of the EVS at
beginnings and middles of sentences are equal to mean
EVSs. The short EVS at sentence endings are not the
cumulative effects of constraints—which would predict large
EVSs—but are habitual responses to the sentence ending,
punctuation, typographical spacing, and capitalization that
mark the start of a new sentence.

Phrases
There is substantial evidence that grammatical phrases behave as units in various psychological tasks. The units may
be formed by the intonation contours of phrases or the
meaning units that often are contained in phrases. In fact,
the expression that reading occurs in "meaning units"
(Buswell 1920) might well be expressed today in terms of
phrase structures of sentences. In studies of memory using
the probe technique, subjects took longer to respond when
the two words were separated by a phrase boundary (Blumenthal 1967), and the famous click studies (Fodor and
Bever 1965) show that people hear a click as occurring in a
nearby phrase boundary. It is fashionable to talk of such

findings as demonstrating the "psychological reality of phrases," though McNeill and Lindig (1973), in a superb experiment, showed that, depending on the task, various linguistic units may form the appropriate units for psychological functions.

Schlesinger (1968) was the first researcher to state explicitly that the EVS extended to phrase boundaries, a finding since confirmed by many others (Levin and Turner 1968; Levin and Kaplan 1968; Rode 1974–1975). He wrote that "the span of the eyes . . . ahead of the voice represents a unit of decoding."[2] He predicted that the units of reading could be defined in terms of syntactic structure so that his subjects (adult readers of Hebrew) would read ahead to the end of a group of words that could exist alone as a unit or phrase. He found that readers tended to end their EVSs at the ends of units, chains, or phrases, which are syntactic and semantic "wholes." One such study by Levin and Turner (1968) will be described in detail to show how this finding came about.

The study was designed to investigate the effects of sentence structure on the EVS, as well as the developmental course of such effects. Ten subjects at each of six grade levels were studied: second, fourth, sixth, eighth, tenth, and adults (college students). Four types of sentences were used:

1. Active sentences made up of *two-word* phrases entirely;
2. Active sentences made up of *three-word* phrases;
3. Passive sentences made up of *three-word* phrases;
4. Active sentences made up of *four-word* phrases.

The number of sentences within each of the four types was such that the light could be turned off at all possible

between-word points in the first two phrases. The light was
turned off an equal number of times before and after the first
major grammatical break of the sentence, that is, between
the main noun phrase and the main verb phrase. The research materials for two-word phrases are illustrated
schematically in figure 7.1. A different sentence was used for
each of the light-out positions. Thus, there were 8 two-word,
12 three-word active, 12 three-word passive, and 16 four-
word active sentences, in addition to 8 structureless word
lists. The total number of presentations was 56.

Sentences were devised to contain enough phrase units so
that there would always be at least ten words in the sentences beyond the light-out position. For children in grades
six or beyond, the critical sentences were part of four-
sentence paragraphs. The critical sentence was the first, second, third, or fourth an equal number of times. For the second and fourth graders, the paragraphs contained two sentences, and the critical sentence occurred in either the first
or second position. If the critical sentence were always in
the same position in the paragraph (e.g., always the second),
there was the danger that some subjects would see the pattern and scan ahead an abnormally long distance on just
those sentences. The sentences were randomized, and the
same order was used for each subject.

Two sets of sentences were used. One set, containing
second-grade vocabulary, was used with the second and
fourth graders; another was made up with sixth-grade
vocabulary, was used with the sixth grade and all older
subjects.

This study differed from most others in that recognition
lists were made up for half of the sentences in each of the

/ 1   2   3   4

  1 / 2   3   4

  1   2 / 3   4

  1   2   3 / 4

  1   2   3   4

  1   2   3   4

  1   2   3   4

  1   2   3   4

Break between main noun and verb phrases

  5   6   7   8

  5   6   7   8

  5   6   7   8

  5   6   7   8

/ 5   6   7   8

  5 / 6   7   8

  5   6 / 7   8

  5   6   7 / 8

/ = light out position

7.1
Schematic of sentences made up
of two-word phrases, with
light-out positions (Levin and
Turner 1968).

four sentence types. Each recognition list contained five content words (omitting, for example, *a, the, by, to,* etc.) from the final part of the sentence, starting three words beyond the light-out position, and five distractors, one for each of the real content words.

The apparatus was simple: the text was placed behind a window in a slant-topped box and was visible only when a light inside the box was turned on. The experimenter controlled the light, and a timer was started when the light was turned on and stopped when it went off, thus providing a measure of reading rate.

The subject was instructed to look at a red dot on the window of the apparatus, which marked the point where the beginning of the paragraph would appear when the light was turned on. We thought by this means to reduce the reader's tendency to scan ahead before starting to read aloud. The subject was told to read at normal rate, the rate at which he or she would read a storybook aloud. When the light went out, the reader was told to report all words seen beyond the word being said when the text became unavailable. When there was a recognition list for the sentence, the subject was shown each word of the list individually and was asked if it had been seen.

We will have occasion to return to this experiment when we take up the active-passive voice in sentences and the effects of phrase length. First, we ask of this study whether there is a tendency to report EVSs that end at phrase boundaries. Simply counting the number of times that the reported EVS ended at a phrase boundary has the danger of introducing a serious artifact. Suppose that a reader has a usual EVS of three words. On some sentences the reader's modal EVS will take him or her to the end of phrases, uninfluenced by the grammar of the sentence. One of two corrections should be made. First, a reader's modal EVS and the number of times the reader would have read to the end of a phrase may be calculated by subtracting his mode from the total number of times the EVS coincided with phrase endings. If it were the case that subjects tended to read to the end of phrase units only when their usual EVS ended there, the sum of all the scores computed as described above would be zero.

Another way of testing the hypothesis that subjects tended to read to the end of phrase boundaries more frequently than to nonboundary positions is to compare the number of times subjects read to phrase boundaries with the number of times they read to nonboundary positions and to divide by the number of chances to read to nonboundary positions in the phrase. Thus, in the case of the three-word phrases, there would be one chance to stop at a phrase boundary for every two nonphrase boundaries. Assuming 10 readings to boundaries and 2 to nonboundaries, the calculation would be $(10-2)/2=4$.

In this experiment, the first calculation tells us that the overall mean number of times subjects read to phrase boundaries, over and above the times they read to phrase boundaries with their modal EVS, was 8.20, which is significantly greater than zero.

The second calculation, an overall comparison of boundary versus nonboundary reading, showed that subjects read to boundaries significantly more times than to nonboundaries. Each type of calculation tells us something different, though the evidence for the EVS's responsiveness to the phrase structure of the sentences is clear.

The phenomenon of reading to phrase (or clause boundaries) is now widely replicated. Schlesinger (1968) found it with adult readers of Hebrew; Levin and Turner (1967) with a wide age range of subjects reading English; Levin and Kaplan (1968) with adults; Resnick (1970) with children and adults; Rode (1974–1975) with children; and Vazquez, Glucksberg, and Danks (1977–1978) with adults. Of these, Rode and Vazquez, Glucksberg, and Danks were concerned with clause boundaries and merit detailed discussion below.

Pseudoboundaries and Reading Errors

In addition to reading to phrase boundaries, subjects in the Levin and Turner study changed either the sentence structure or the last word reported in the EVS in such a way as to make a phrase boundary. For example, if the final part of the phrase was ". . . next to the house," some subjects might read ". . . next door." Schlesinger (1968) also found such "errors to form reasonable 'chains'."

Rode (1974–1975) reports the following example. The target sentence was "Golden wheat grew very high and tall green corn was planted." When the light-out position was after "grew," 68 percent of the children read "golden wheat grew very high and tall," a perfectly acceptable phrase-ending EVS. Rode also accepted "good" errors in calculating a second EVS score and found that third, fourth, and fifth graders read "cereal" for "oatmeal," "cooked" for "grilled," and "not angry" for "very pleased."

This tendency for reading errors to retain a text that is

grammatically correct and meaningful, though possibly different from the original text's meaning, is characteristic of readers from the time they begin to learn to read (Weber 1970), as well as for adult readers (Kolers 1970).

Critical Positions and Length of Phrases

As we saw in the discussion of Buswell's and Fairbanks's research, the sizes of the EVSs in various parts of the sentence are not very informative unless we consider the grammatical nature of the sentences. Nevertheless, several recent experiments varied the length of phrases in the text and the positions of the light-out points. They will be taken up here, while the bulk of the work on critical positions and phrase length will be covered in the next chapter, where they will be considered together with the specific types of sentences.

Levin and Turner's subjects read sentences composed entirely of phrases that were two, three, or four words long. The critical positions are illustrated in figure 7.1. The size of the EVSs for all ages other than the second graders was strongly influenced by phrase length. The results are illustrated in figures 7.2 and 7.3. The EVSs are longest for those sentences made up of three-word phrases. A possible explanation runs like this: if the subject is reading in phrase groups in a sentence made up of four-word phrases and the light is turned off before or after the first word in a phrase, the subject would have to read either four or eight (or three or seven) words to reach a phrase boundary. Seven or eight words most likely would be beyond the subject's EVS *and* the elastic limits of the EVS. Therefore, the subject would probably shrink the EVS by one or two words and read only to the end of the nearest phrase boundary. Since the longest

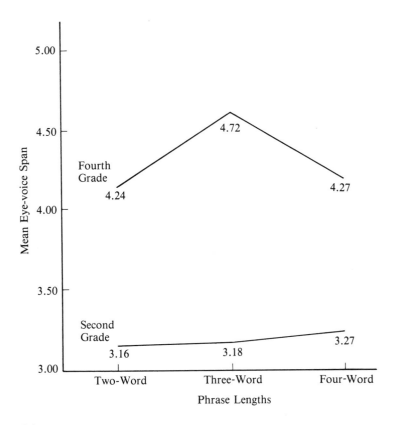

7.2
Second- and fourth-grade EVSs,
by phrase length (Levin and
Turner 1968).

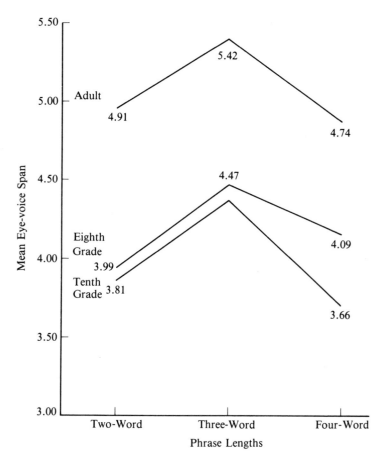

7.3
Eighth-grade, tenth-grade, and
adult EVSs by phrase length
(Levin and Turner 1968).

two-phrase sequences in a three-word phrase sentence would
be six words (much nearer the usual EVS of most readers),
it is more likely that the reader would stretch the EVS to
take in the two phrases rather than shrink the EVS to take
in two or three words. In the two-word phrase sentences the
longest sequence for two phrases would be an easily handle-

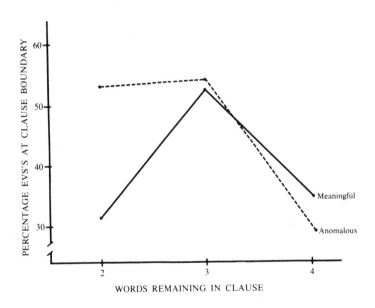

7.4
Mean percentage of EVSs coinciding with a clause boundary,
as a function of semantic constraint and the number of words
between the interruption and the
next clause boundary (Vazquez,
Glucksberg, and Danks 1977–
1978).

able four words. Phrase length had little influence on the EVSs of second graders, who read to phrase boundaries less often than did older subjects; this once more suggests that beginning readers are less able to exploit grammatical and semantic constraints in their reading than older readers.

There are several confirmations of this explanation. Rode (1974–1975) found that for various age groups, the number of words (two or three) in the phrase influenced whether or not subjects stopped reading at a particular boundary. Vazquez, Glucksberg, and Danks (1977–1978) plotted the number of words remaining in a clause with the probability of EVSs ending at clause boundaries. Their results are presented in figure 7.4. The chances of reading to a grammatical boundary are clearly highest when three, compared to two or four, words remain in the clause.

From these several lines of evidence, the size of the EVS depends to some extent on the sizes of phrases, and size is effective because of the tendency to read to grammatical boundaries.

8

THE EVS
AND
TYPES OF
SENTENCES

In this chapter we present the evidence most critical to our interpretation of the EVS. Spans are longest on the more constrained textual materials, and there is strong evidence that constraints facilitate recognition. Consequently, when faced with grammatically constrained materials readers can recognize the constituent parts more efficiently, probably through fewer and briefer fixations of the eyes on the text. To build this argument further, constraints vary within sentences, and their ends are usually more constrained than their beginnings. Moreover, some grammatical forms are more constrained than others. For example, we will review the EVSs on noun phrases versus verb phrases because we know that one is a more constrained form than the other. We will compare active and passive sentences since they are differently constrained. Likewise, the contrast between left- and right-embedded sentences will be discussed. Finally, we will take up the small amount of evidence that exists about semantic constraints.

Phrase Length

It is reasonable to assume that constraints of grammar are higher *within* phrases and clauses than *between* phrases and clauses. We have had occasion to show that this assumption explains various psychological functions such as memory for and perception of verbal materials, as well as the tendency to report EVSs that extend to phrase boundaries (see ch. 7).

If within-clause constraints are stronger than those between clauses, the removal of text after the subject has read several words should yield longer EVSs than when the reader's voice is at a clause boundary (Vazquez, Glucksberg, and Danks 1977–1978). The materials were designed so that under either condition two, three, or four words remained to the next clause boundary. EVSs were longer when the interruptions occurred *within* a clause. However, the effect was not robust, since the major finding appeared only when three words remained in the clause (see fig. 7.4). Within-clause breaks yielded a higher incidence of completing EVSs at clause boundaries, again modified by the number of words in the clause.

Levin and Jones (1968) only partially confirmed these results, though the experimental conditions differed slightly. The target sentences, containing phrase lengths of four or five words, were either in the active or passive voice. The critical light-off conditions were in the medial position of the phrase or on the final word of the phrase. First, EVSs were longer on the four-word than the five-word phrases, as can be seen in table 8.1. Second, EVSs were longer when the

Table 8.1
Mean EVS (words) for various conditions
(after Levin and Jones 1968)

Active = 4.32		Passive = 4.36	
Phrase Length			
4 word = 4.10	5 word = 3.63	4 word = 4.92	5 word = 3.78
Position		Position	
M = 4.33	M = 3.89	M = 4.41	M = 3.17
T = 5.66	T = 3.41	T = 5.44	T = 4.43

light was turned off on a phrase-terminal[1] word than in the
middle. That is, four-word phrases with the critical position
at the phrase boundary yielded the longest EVS. The likely
explanation is that when the voice is ending a phrase, the
eyes are well into the next phrase, and, if the size is not out
of reach (four versus five words), the reader reports more
text. At the medial position the EVSs are shorter, though
there is a strong tendency to report phrase-ending EVSs
when the critical position is in the middle of the phrase. This
last finding is congruent with Vazquez, Glucksberg, and
Danks (1977–1978).

Another part of the Levin and Jones study involved the
reading of active sentences constructed on the following
model:

1st Phrase	2nd Phrase	Prepositional Phrase
(W1 W2 W3 W4)	(W1 W2 W3 W4)	(W1 W2 W3)
3rd Phrase	Final Phrase	
(W1 W2 W3 W4)	(W1 W2 W3 W4)	

The data about the phrase in the sentences that contain the critical point is very clear. When the light went out in the first phrase, the EVS was 3.42 words, 4.29 words for the second phrase, and 5.5 words for the third phrase. These means differ significantly. The results are another clear demonstration, if another is needed, that the constraints are stronger at the ends than the beginnings of sentences (Kolers 1950), and the constraints appear to increase in a monotonic fashion. A related finding is the number of times the subjects' EVSs ended at phrase boundaries. Out of 72 opportunities, subjects reported to boundaries 26 times in the first phrase, 38/72 in the second phrase, and 54/72 in the third phrase. In no case did subjects read beyond the immediate phrase to the end of the next phrase, when the light went out at the beginning of the first phrase. In only 4 of the 38 sentences read to phrase boundaries did the subjects read to the end of the next phrase, when the critical position was the start of the second phrase (3 of the 4 instances were by the same person). But when the light went out at the beginning of the third phrase, readers extended their EVSs to the end of the next phrase—the end of the sentences—28 times. This is a powerful demonstration that constraints were greatest in the final part of the sentences *and* that readers were influenced by their attempts to achieve the full meaning of the sentence. Rode (1974–1975) below makes a similar case that clauses, as larger units of meaning than phrases, are operative units in reading.

One other part of Levin's and Jones's study is germane to this issue. Spaces between words were filled by asterisks (*) at various points in the sentence. We shall consider only three instances where the filler was placed in the spaces between phrases. Filling all of the spaces between words badly disrupts reading. First, filling the spaces before the first word of the first phrase effectively shrinks the EVS. Second, filling the space that is the boundary between the first and second phrases substantially curtails the EVS. Third, and most significant, obliterating the space between the second and third phrases has *little* effect on the EVS. Apparently, within-sentence constraints in this part of the sentence are strong enough to overcome the distractions of the filled interword space, which normally would have reduced the EVS.

Noun Phrases and Verb Phrases

Rode (1974–1975) has argued, correctly in our opinion, that young—second and third grade—children's inability to use the constraints of passive sentences (Levin and Turner 1968) may not reflect their inability to make use of grammatical structure but simply may represent their lack of experience with the passive voice (e.g., Grossman 1969). Passive sentences hardly ever appear in books used during the early elementary-school grades. On the other hand, conjoined sentences of noun and verb phrases are common reading fare for young children, so these simple forms may be more revealing about young readers' use of grammar to form higher-order units. Rode employed the following kinds of sentences in an EVS experiment with third-, fourth-, and fifth-grade children:

Type A. These sentences consisted of a two-word noun phrase, three-word verb phrases, conjunction, three-word noun phrase, and a two-word verb phrase. Big/hamburgers were/slowly fried and then/hot dogs were grilled.

Type B. These sentences consisted of a three-word phrase, two-word phrase, conjunction, two-word noun phrase, and a three-word verb phrase. Little/round eggs are/colored and candy/bunnies taste very good.

(Critical, light-out positions are indicated by /.)

When the text was removed in the noun phrase, the EVSs were longer for all three age groups. Rode interprets these results as a striving, by the expansion of the EVS, to take in units that made sense. Completing the noun phrase provides minimal information, as can be seen in the examples. "The information or completeness of thought gained from an initial noun phrase is minimal, and it is only upon reading the verb phrase that the reader knows what sentential meaning the author intended. This striving for sentence-length units would, in the present experiment, tend to lengthen the EVS for stopping points in the initial noun phrase and constrict it for points in the verb phrase" (p. 137). Further, if an EVS score is based on meaningful completions by the readers, even though the words were not actually present in the text, the tendency to expand to sentencelike units is even more marked. Rode believes, as do Vazquez, Glucksberg, and Danks (1977–1978), a clause, which is sententially more complete than a phrase, is "the unit which readers attempt to decode." This tendency, while clear for all age groups, is clearer with older children. It is important to note that readers as young as third graders gave evidence of using grammar and meaning in reading sentences of the kinds they had seen often in their school readers. That very young children are aware of the unitizing function of grammar is clear from the finding that even second graders report longer EVSs on sentences than on word lists. However, Rode's

results must be seen in the context of the sentence types
and critical positions. The short noun phrases allowed the
readers to pick up some of the words in the equally brief
verb phrases. Removing the text when the reader's voice was
in the verb phrase, the conjunction, and then the end of
the sentence effectively truncated the number of words the
children reported. The latter point is demonstrated in Levin
and Turner's (1968) results. For second and fourth graders
the EVS in active sentences were longer *after* than before
the main verb. Their sentences contained a substantial
number of words after the verb, thereby permitting longer
EVSs than did Rode's sentences.

Active and Passive Sentences
The essential ingredients for research on the EVS within
sentences of specific grammatical types are, first, determina-
tion of constraints within the sentences, and, second, the
measurement of the EVSs at various critical points. Fortu-
nately, a constraint analysis existed for active and passive
sentences. As we will see, the study of grammatically embedded sentences entailed learning the nature of the constraints in those types of sentences.

Clark (1965) had reported that the pattern of contingencies
between major sentence parts is quite different for active
and passive sentences. His subjects generated sentences
from active and passive sentence frames from which two or
three of the major sentence parts (the actor, verb, or object)
had been deleted. An uncertainty analysis of the results
yielded a measure of both the diversity of completions for
each of the sentence parts and the extent to which the parts
of the sentences covaried. The uncertainties associated with

the actors, verbs, and objects and the pattern of constraints between them were found to be different for active and passive sentences. The directionality of the constraints within the two kinds of sentences are diagramed in figure 8.1. The arrowheads represent the directions of constraints. The verb constrains the object and the object constrains the verb in both active and passive sentences. The important finding is that the latter part of passive sentences, the verb and the actor, is highly constrained by the first part, the object; this was not true for corresponding parts of active sentences.

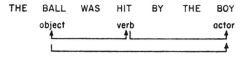

ACTIVE SENTENCE:

THE	BOY	HIT	THE	BALL
	actor	verb		object

PASSIVE SENTENCE:

THE	BALL	WAS	HIT	BY	THE	BOY
	object		verb			actor

8.1
Directionality of the constraint between sentence parts (Clark 1965).

The right-hand part of active sentences, the verb and object, were relatively independent of the first part, the actor. As a validation of this analysis, Clark (1966) later showed that recall for different sentence parts could be predicted from these uncertainties and contingencies.

We expected, therefore, that if the EVS were sensitive to within-sentence constraints, the span should increase toward the middle of the passive sentences, but there should not be a corresponding increase in the active forms. Said more precisely, the EVS should increase in size when the reader reaches information that specifies that the sentence is in the passive voice. Although this information is signaled partly by the nature of the verb phrase, explicit confirmation comes only when the "eye" reaches the "by" phrase. There is no reason to believe that the reader has firm evidence that he is reading a passive sentence prior to either of these phrases.

In one study (Levin and Kaplan 1968), the subjects were 18 college students. Besides the comparison of active and passive sentences, each type was composed of either four-word or five-word phrases, since the evidence is strong that with the tendency for the EVS to extend to phrase boundaries the length of phrases must be taken into account. The four types of sentences used in this experiment were:

1. Active sentences composed of four-word phrases.
2. Passive sentences composed of four-word phrases.
3. Active sentences composed of five-word phrases.
4. Passive sentences composed of five-word phrases.

The four-word sentences contained 19 words, made up of five phrases of these lengths: 4 words, 4 words, 3 words, 4 words, 4 words. The five-word sentences contained 18 words divided into four phrases: 5 words, 5 words, 3 words, 5 words. The short three-word phrase represented the "by + agent" phrase in the passive sentences and a prepositional phrase in the active sentences. The sentences were designed so that the first half of both active and passive sentences were structurally similar. For example:

Passives: The cute chubby/boy/was/slowly/being/wheeled/by the maid along the narrow lane to the country store.

The strange opinionated/army/officer/was/firmly/and /forcefully/persuaded/by his superiors to inform every enlisted soldier.

Actives: The brash tall/man/was/certainly/being/loud/at the meeting of the new group on the main campus.

The happy boisterous/drunken/glutton/was/trying/hard/to /behave/at the dinner of the exclusive gourmet club.

Each sentence was embedded in a separate paragraph of four or five unrelated sentences. Since exploratory data indicated that subjects often scanned the first line before beginning to read aloud, the target sentence was never first, but it could occur in any other position in the paragraph.

The EVS was systematically measured at numerous critical positions within the set of target sentences. EVS scores were obtained after the third word and every succeeding word up to the "by phrase" in the passives and the corresponding point in the prepositional phrases of the active sentences. The critical, light-out, positions are indicated by / in the above examples. There were four sentences for each critical position. The target sentences were arranged so that there were at least three words preceding the critical word on the same line. At least eleven words succeeded the critical word for the four-word sentences, and eight succeeded it for the five-word sentences. Few readers extended their EVSs to the last word in the sentence.

The paragraphs were exposed on a small, ground-glass, rear-projection screen placed directly in front of the subject, so the lines could be read with minimal head movements. The size of the projected letters was approximately equivalent to that found in texts. A fixation point, indicating where the beginning of each paragraph would appear, eliminated the problem of having the subject search the screen each time a new paragraph was exposed.

Subjects were instructed to read aloud at their normal reading rate. When the reader's voice reached the critical position in the sentence, the projector shutter was closed to remove the material from view. The EVS score was the number of correct words reported.

The results for the sentences made up of four-word phrases are presented in figure 8.2 and those for five-word phrases are in figure 8.3. The overall average EVS for the four-word sentences is 4.5 words, for the five-word sentences it is 4.0 words. These two means reconfirm our findings that EVSs are longest on intermediate-size phrases. For both phrase lengths the differences in EVSs for active compared to passive sentences strongly confirm our hypotheses. Several comparisons are interesting. In the active sentences the mean EVSs for each of the critical positions do not differ from each other; that is, the EVS curve for active sentences is essentially a straight, horizontal line. The passives present quite different pictures. For the four-word sentences positions 1 through 4 do not differ from each other

120

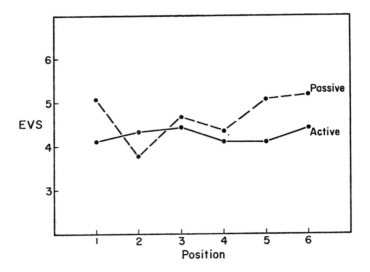

8.2
Mean EVS for various critical
positions in four-word phrase
active and passive sentences
(Levin and Kaplan 1968).

but do differ from positions 5 and 6 (p < 0.01). For five-
word passive sentences positions 1 through 6 are significantly different from positions 7 and 8 (p < 0.01). Finally,
when we compare the active and passive curves in both
figures, the EVSs in the passive sentences are significantly
longer than in the active sentences *only on the last two critical positions* (p < 0.01).

To sum up, the findings are: (1) in sentences composed of
four- and five-word phrases, the EVS is longer for the
passives at the two terminal critical positions than for the ac-

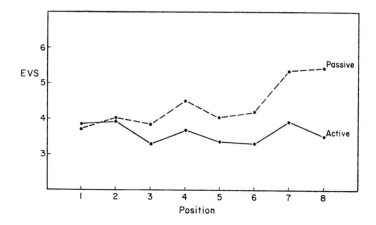

8.3
Mean EVS for various critical
positions in five-word phrase active and passive sentences (Levin and Kaplan 1968).

tives; (2) within the active sentences, the position at which
the text was removed had no effect on the EVS; and (3) in
the passive sentences, the EVS at the two final positions
was larger than at critical positions earlier in the sentence.
These findings suggest the tenability of the major hypothesis
that the EVS varies in accordance with intrasentence constraints. The results show that the EVS is longer for passive
sentences at that point where the active and passive forms
begin to be differentially constrained (Clark 1965). Since the
first portions of both active and passive sentences were identical and the short three-word phrase in the active sentences
was a prepositional phrase where the contingencies within
the phrase itself would not be expected to differ from those

within the passive "by + agent" phrase, the differences must be attributed to the structure of the sentence as a whole. Further, these differences appear precisely when the eye would have picked up the "by + agent," the interpretation of which was critical for the total sentence. Finally, it should be pointed out again that this experiment provided strong evidence for the general finding that the EVS tended to terminate at phrase boundaries.

Other experiments that compared the reading of active and passive sentences did not always confirm the study and in some instances yielded results that are difficult to reconcile with Levin's and Kaplan's. The study by Levin and Turner (1968) has already been described in detail. Among other purposes this study compared the EVSs on active and passive sentences as read by subjects of various ages. Four types of sentences were used:

1. Active sentences made up of *two-word* phrases entirely;
2. Active sentences made up of *three-word* phrases;
3. Passive sentences made up of *three-word* phrases;
4. Active sentences made up of *four-word* phrases.

Second and fourth graders, since they read the same sentences, were analyzed together, as were the subjects in the eighth and tenth grades and the adults.[2] For the younger readers the EVS tended to be longer before the verb in the passive sentences and after the verb in active sentences, though, as can be seen in figure 8.4, the major differences on the EVS occur before the verb; after the verb the EVSs appear to be about the same length. For the older subjects, the overall mean EVS was longer for the passive than the active sentences. However, as with the younger readers, the EVS

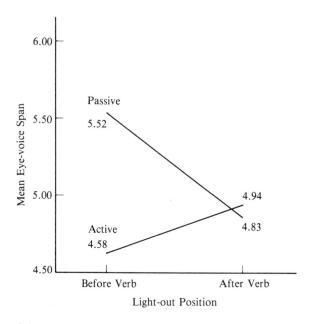

8.4
Mean EVS for second and
fourth grades, by critical position and sentence voice (Levin
and Turner 1968).

was longer before the verb in the passive sentences and after
the verb in the active sentences. (See figure 8.5).

There is little evidence in this study and others (Grossman
1969) that children below the fourth grade systematically
exploit knowledge of grammar in their reading and in speech
production the passive voice appears late in language development. The longer EVS in passive sentences confirms
the Levin and Kaplan study. Longer EVSs toward the ends
of active sentences are expected (Levin and Jones 1968).

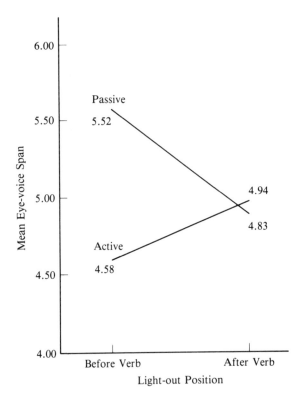

8.5
Mean EVS for eighth and tenth
grades and adults, by critical
position and sentence voice
(Levin and Turner 1968).

However, long EVSs in the early parts of passive sentences are difficult to explain. Compared to the experiment devoted entirely to the active-passive comparison (Levin and Kaplan 1968), Levin and Turner's sentences were shorter and less complicated. It may be that the eyes were farther into the sentence when the text was removed prior to the voicing of the main verb. A reconciliation of the studies would entail a detailed analysis of each critical position rather than the gross grouping, before versus after, the main verb.

A partial confirmation of the original active-passive finding was reported by Levin and Jones (1968). This study was designed primarily to investigate the effects of filling the interword spaces at critical points in the sentence to observe the effects on the EVS. Control sentences were printed with normal word spacing, and both active and passive sentences were included. The mean EVS for actives was 3.4 words and for passives was 4.4 words. The difference is statistically significant ($p < .001$). However, the difference occurred only when the subjects (adults) were reading sentences composed of five-word phrases; four-word phrase sentences revealed no active-passive differences. Again, the reason for such partial findings is not clear.

In summary, what can be said about the EVS in active and passive sentences? An experiment to test the specific points in active and passive sentences where a constraint analysis predicted divergence in the EVSs yielded unequivocal results with adults. Other studies, which tested the active-passive distinctions peripheral to other purposes, were less clear. Children do not use these constraints in reading. Overall, the EVS is longer for passive than for active sentences.

Right- and Left-Embedded Sentences

Though somewhat confirmatory, these findings, based on only two types of sentences—simple actives and passives— provide a slim foundation on which to rest the generalization that those parts of sentences that are more highly constrained grammatically are read in larger units than less-constrained sentence forms. Consequently, Levin, Grossman, Kaplan, and Yang (1972) tested the same hypotheses by comparing left- and right-embedded sentences. Left-embedded (LE) sentences contain adjectival modifiers between the subject and the main verb of the sentences; right-embedded (RE) have the modifiers in the predicate, that is, in the verb phrase of the sentence. A simple LE sentence is, "The cake that she made won the prize"; in RE form it reads, "She made the cake that won the prize."

Unlike the earlier study of actives and passives, no analysis of constraints existed for RE and LE sentences; such an analysis had to be undertaken as the first stage of the study. A modified cloze procedure was used for the constraint analysis. In a standard cloze task (Taylor 1953) single words are deleted from a text and subjects are asked to supply the missing word. From the number of different words filled in by a group of subjects an estimate of constraints within the frame can be calculated. However, we were interested in the predictability of grammatical forms within the sentence, rather than the predictability of *one* word in a particular grammatical frame. Hence, it was necessary to delete segments larger than a single word. Because of our interest in structural rather than lexical variability the responses to the blanks were categorized by equivalent or nonequivalent

grammatical types. Constraints were estimated from the
number of different grammatical types found in this manner.

The size and position of deletions were varied to include
almost as many combinations as were possible. Nine different frames were used for each type of sentence. These are illustrated in figure 8.6 with two sample sentences. Three test
booklets composed of one sentence of each type of frame
were compiled in randomized orders, a different order for
each booklet. A blank for each word indicated the number of
words to fill in. There was one sentence per page in order to
minimize response bias.

The subjects—68 undergraduate students—were instructed
to complete the sentences in any way they wished, as long
as the finished sentence was grammatical. Only grammatically correct responses were analyzed. The acceptable responses were categorized by grammatical type. Average uncertainties were computed for each frame using Shannon's
procedure (outlined in Garner 1962, pp. 20–24) in which
$U(x) = -\mathrm{E}p(x) \log p(x)$. Essentially, this procedure weights
the various types obtained by their frequency of occurrence.
The result is expressed in *bits* of information; the more bits
associated within a given frame, the greater the uncertainty.

The average uncertainties within each frame are shown in
figure 8.6. Frames III and IV, where all or part of the embedded phrase was omitted with the rest of the sentence left
intact, are particularly interesting. When the entire embedded phrase was deleted (frame III), RE sentences were
more constrained than LE by 1.03 bits. When the first word
of the embedding was given, differences were reduced to
slightly over 0.5 bits. In general, this pattern held for all
comparable RE and LE frames. Equal uncertainties occurred

128

RIGHT EMBEDDED FRAMES

The soldier remembered the prayer that the priest gave during the morning service.

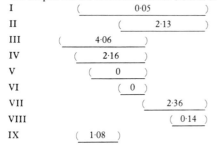

I	(5·38)
II	(3·39)
III	(3·04)
IV	(1·48)
V	(0)
VI	(0)
VII	(0·77)
VIII	(0)
IX	(0·84)

LEFT EMBEDDED FRAMES

The sculptor that the church hired carved the altar in the new chapel.

I	(0·05)
II	(2·13)
III	(4·06)
IV	(2·16)
V	(0)
VI	(0)
VII	(2·36)
VIII	(0·14)
IX	(1·08)

8.6
Sample sentences showing the locations of deletions and average uncertainties (Levin, Grossman, Kaplan, and Yang 1972).

only when no grammatical variability was possible (e.g., LE frame VI, where only a verb could be filled in).

When the frames were such that constructions other than embeddings were possible, embedded completions were more frequent in RE than in LE frames. For example, when only the embedded phrase was omitted, 78 percent of the responses to RE frames were embeddings; corresponding LE frames produced 33 percent. One frame type (labeled RE I for convenience) consisted of only an initial noun phrase and two prepositional phrases separated by seven blanks. Here, subjects could produce either LE or RE sentences. Again, of the 34 percent embedded responses, 77 percent were RE and only 23 percent were LE.

Not only were RE constructions more frequent, but the forms they took were less variable. A constraint analysis, this time analyzing only embedded responses occurring in frame III, gave average uncertainties of 1.5 and 3.25 for RE and LE, respectively—a difference of 1.75 bits. In summary, there are demonstrable differences in the constraints in RE and LE sentences. Embedded phrases after the main verb were more frequent than before it and were more constrained in form. If the constraint model of sentence reading is correct, longer EVSs should occur in RE sentences.

Two experiments, which replicated each other very closely, will be described. Examples of the two types of sentences with the critical positions indicated by / are:

LE: Before he died/the gangster/that/the police/shot/closed/the/door/of the room near the kitchen.

RE: After the meeting/the janitor/found/the magazine/that/the/woman/left/on the chair in the hall.

The form of the sentence in the constraint analysis (see fig. 8.6) left one possibly important factor uncontrolled: the embedded phrase in RE sentences occurred three words later than in LE sentences. Since there is substantial evidence that the EVS increases with distance read into the sentence, a longer span in the embedded region of RE sentences might be interpreted as a position effect. Therefore, an initial three-word prepositional phrase was added to LE sentences—*before he died,* in the example above—in order to equate the position of the embedded phrase in both types of sentences.

In the first experiment four sentences for each critical position were used. The subjects were 10 undergraduate students. The target sentences were in a paragraph of unrelated sentences that were back-projected onto a ground-glass screen. The position of the sentence in the paragraph line was adjusted so that there would always be at least nine words following the light-out position on the same line.

Mean EVSs for each critical position are shown in figure 8.7. The grammatical function of the word immediately preceding the critical position is also indicated. EVSs in RE sentences were longer than in LE sentences, as expected. In fact, curves for RE and LE sentences began to diverge by the second critical position. The span in LE sentences continued to drop with successive critical positions, reaching its lowest point in the middle of the embedded phrase, and began to rise in the region of the verb of the embedded phrase (position 5); the rise accompanying the main verb actually began when the embedded verb was reached. While the RE curve does dip in the middle of the embedded phrase (position 6), it rose again before the end of the embedded

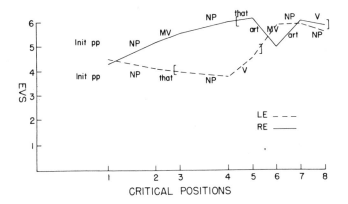

8.7
Mean EVS by critical positions
for RE and LE sentences (Levin, Grossman, Kaplan, and
Yang 1972).

phrase, with positions 7 and 8 producing virtually identical
EVSs for both types of sentences.

A three-way analysis of variance (subjects, sentence type,
and critical position) indicated that the main effects for sentence type and critical position were significant (p. < 0.001).
RE sentences yielded longer EVSs than LE sentences; the
EVS increased with successive critical positions. In addition,
the interaction between critical position and sentence type
was significant (p < 0.001), indicating the crisscross of the
curves after the sixth critical position.

The above experiment was replicated with a larger number
of subjects—22 undergraduates—and with the addition of
two more random orders in which the sentences were presented. Figure 8.8 shows the results in graphic form. The

132

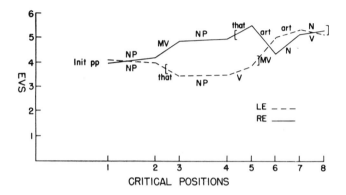

8.8
Mean EVS by critical positions
for RE and LE sentences: rep-
lication (Levin, Grossman, Kaplan, and Yang 1972).

curves are very similar to those in figure 8.7, and the statistical analyses yielded results exactly comparable to the earlier study.

These findings on right and left embeddings provide the
strongest test of our hypotheses about grammatical constraints within sentences and EVSs. Because of the replica-
tion we may consider the results stable and trustworthy. The
constraints were independently determined, and the same
sentences on which the constraints were measured were
used to measure the EVSs.

There is no evidence, however, that elementary-school
children are able to use the constraints in embedded sentences (Grossman 1969). Active productive control of these
structures are late to develop in children's languages.

Research Supplementary to Actives-Passives and Embeddings
Long EVSs occur when the text is read rapidly. Rapid reading, in turn, entails long forward eye movements, few fixations, fixations of short duration, and infrequent regressions. Said in the vernacular, the eyes move quickly and smoothly over the page. EVSs are shortened by different kinds of eye movements: short saccades, many and long fixations, and frequent and time-consuming regressions. These findings, carried to more precision, predict that in those constrained parts of sentences that yield long EVSs, the eye movements should be more efficient than on less constrained parts of sentences. Wanat (1971) tested these predictions on active and passive and on right- and left-embedded sentences.

In general, active sentences are read more smoothly than passives. There are fewer and shorter forward fixations by readers of active sentences. Further, there are fewer regressions, and less time is spent on regressions in active than passive sentences. Thus far, the results of eye-movement measurements do not confirm the longer EVSs on passive sentences. However, the EVSs were longer in the area of the passive sentences' agentive phrases compared to the actives' prepositional phrases (Levin and Kaplan 1968). Wanat reported more regressive movements and time spent on regressions in this area of passive sentences compared to spatially analogous areas of active sentences. These differences appear graphically in figure 8.9. In summary, we may conclude that eye-movement studies only modestly confirm the EVS results on the reading of active and passive sentences.

The results of Wanat's study of eye movements for RE and LE sentences are more in line with the EVS findings.

+AGC The ship was beached by the helper in the storm.

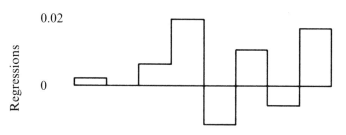

ACT   The poet was writing in the studio of his home.

8.9
Differences between mean
number of regressions per sentence and areas in active (ACT)
and passive (+AGC) sentences
(Wanat 1971).

There are fewer forward fixations, and less time is spent on forward fixations while reading RE compared to LE sentences. Some of the results are presented in figure 8.10. It is noteworthy that the longest fixation times occur in the areas of the main verbs in both types of sentences. Several investigators have pointed to the importance of the main verb for understanding sentences (Gladney and Kralee 1967; Chafe 1970). RE and LE sentences do not differ in the regressive eye movements they elicit.

We have been guided by the hypothesis that syntactically and semantically constrained structures in text are more easily available to readers. Sawyer (1971) changes the angle of the lens to look at this issue from a different perspective. Suppose, she reasoned, that parts of the text were less available to the reader because of its physical appearance—it is blurred, smudged, or the type is broken, the paper creased. Will such physical impoverishments of the stimulus have milder consequences for highly constrained text? Said another way, if we are required to give less visual attention to constrained text, can we make do when such text yields less physical information?

Sawyer worked with adult readers to whom she exposed sentences containing some perfectly legible and some physically blurred parts. She was able to create eight degrees of blur by typing with eight carbons; the ribbon copy was normally legible, but the eighth carbon copy was practically unreadable. An example of one such series is reproduced in figure 8.11. The blurred parts of the sentence were phrases taken from other studies, such as the "by + agent" phrase in passive sentences compared to a prepositional phrase in active sentences and LE and RE phrases.

+ AGC The ship was beached by the helper in the storm.

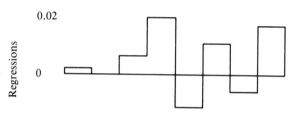

ACT The poet was writing in the studio of his home.

Levin 8.9

LE On the picnic the girls that Bill teased saw the child.

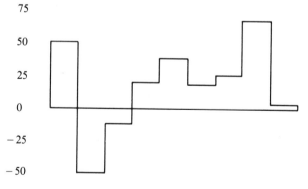

RE The girls saw the child that Bill teased on the picnic.

8.10
Differences between mean time
(in milliseconds) spent in forward fixations and areas in LE
and RE sentences (Wanat 1971).

```
The truck was repaired              ·           at the depot.

The truck was repaired                           at the depot.

The truck was repaired      ·  ·   ·········· at the depot.

 The truck was repaired      ·· ········  at the depot.

 The truck was repaired    ·  the mechanic at the depot.

 The truck was repaired  ··  the mechanic at the depot.

  The truck was repaired by the mechanic at the depot.

  The truck was repaired by the mechanic at the depot.
```

8.11
Sentences with varied degrees
of blur in "*by* + agent" phrases
(Sawyer 1971).

Her findings supplemented other studies in that (1) "by + agent" phrases in passive sentences were recognized under more impoverished conditions than prepositional phrases in active sentences, and (2) the comparison of agent-present and agent-deleted passives did not confirm earlier findings. *By* phrases introducing locatives were more easily recognized than *by* phrases introducing agents. Finally, (3) readers were able to recognize the existence of right embeddings under poorer physical conditions than left embeddings. In general, using a different task than the EVS and eye movements, Sawyer confirmed the interrelationships between grammar and reading.

Semantics and the EVS

Linguists and psychologists are agreed that though language may be analyzed formally into its syntactic and semantic properties, it is more often than not difficult to find a functional separation between these levels of analysis. Speakers and readers certainly will agree that a sequence of words

1. The big black
not only lacks the grammatical requisites of a phrase but also expresses less meaning than

2. The big black bear.
Similarly, Rode (1974–1975) has argued in the examples above that though

3. Big hamburgers

4. were slowly fried
are meaningful phrases, each is not so complete in meaning as

5. Big hamburgers were slowly fried.

Therefore, our earlier discussions of grammar and the EVS were pari passu also discussions of meaning. When Buswell (1920) wrote that the EVS represented a "thought unit" or a "meaning unit," we reasonably interpret him to mean, in more modern vernacular, phrases and/or clauses. Random word lists and low-order statistical approximations to English by definition are devoid of grammatical structure *and* meaning. Children's and adults' reading errors (Weber 1970; Kolers 1970) not only preserve grammaticality but also the meaning of the text, though they may not be precisely what the writer intended. Likewise, insertions in the EVS yield grammatically acceptable and meaningful prose (Schlesinger 1968; Levin and Turner 1968; Rode 1977–1978). Although for our purposes the distinction between grammar and meaning may be arcane, several researchers addressed themselves explicitly to meaning and the EVS; their work will be discussed in this section.

Vazquez, Glucksberg, and Danks (1977–1978) arranged texts of high and low semantic constraint in the following way. College students were given a large number of short paragraphs in which the last sentence was left incomplete and were required to complete them with the first response they thought of. High semantic constraint texts contained the most common responses for each paragraph; under conditions of low semantic constraint the same completions were assigned to other paragraphs. For example,

Since these were not followed by incendiary bombs and the explosion did not start any fires *damage was minimal/we invited friends* though the neighboring buildings were almost demolished.

From this example the anomalous version seems to read like a middle-order statistical approximation to English. The meaningful phrases yielded EVSs substantially longer than anomalous texts. This finding is modified by the clause length (see figure 7.4).

The *understanding* of language—spoken or written—has been a major theoretical concern of transformational grammarians. Linguists and psychologists of this theoretical persuasion make the distinction between the *deep structure* and the *surface structure* of sentences (Katz 1966; Chomsky 1964). Transformationalists maintain that the language user is intuitively aware of differences between deep structure (underlying meaning) and surface structure (the representation of the sentence achieved by applying transformational rules to the deep structure) and that sentences can only be understood by reconstructing their "structural description," including deep structure. Wanat and Levin (1968) tested the suitability of the theoretical distinction between deep and surface structure by an EVS experiment. Two kinds of passive sentences were studied. In the first type the "agent" or "actor" was included, while in the second the agent was deleted. For example:

(1) His brother was beaten up by the gang.

(2) His brother was beaten up by the park.

Both (1) and (2) contain the same words except for one.

However, the substitution of "park" for "gang" reflects a change in the deep structure, that is, the semantics of the sentence. In (1), "gang" is the agent. In both (1) and (2), "his brother" is the object of the verb "beat up." Thus, (1) can be paraphrased as "The gang beat up his brother," whereas (2) obviously cannot be paraphrased as "The park beat up his brother." An appropriate paraphrase would be: His brother was beaten up *near* the park." In (2), the reader must know that "the park" is not the agent and that the action of beating was performed by some agent not specified in the sentence. The agent was *deleted*. Wanat (1971) explains the rationale for shorter EVSs in the agent-deleted passives:

While the number of lexical items is the same in both sentences, the underlying structures are different, and the agent-deleted form is more difficult to process since it conveys more information. That is, the underlying structure of the agent-deleted form consists of OBJECT + VERB + AGENT = ADVERBIAL . . . , the underlying structure of the agent-included form consists of OBJECT + VERB + AGENT. (p. 32)

Type (2) is more difcult because the deep structure requires an agent that is not realized in the surface form of the sentences and an adverbial phrase (place of the beating).

The subjects of the study were 30 college students. Each read eight sentences of type (1) and eight of type (2), in two separate sessions. The sentences were longer than the paradigms given to provide ample words for the EVS after the light-out position. The sentences were put into paragraphs; there were a large number of ''filler'' sentences so that the subjects would not realize that these two types of sentences were the focus of the experiment. In half of the sentences the critical position was immediately prior to the word that reflected a change in the underlying structure (*gang, park*); for the other half the critical position was three words prior to this word.

When the light was turned out immediately before the critical word, the average EVS for the agent-included (type 1) sentences was 5.81 words; for the agent-deleted it was 5.21 words. The difference is statistically significant (p. < .002). When the light-out position was three words prior to the critical word, the EVS differences were in the same direction, though not significant. When the voice was three words away from the word signaling the complexity of meaning, some readers' eyes had reached the critical area of the sentence but had not started to resolve it. When the voice was at the critical word, the eyes showed a reduced span because of having just encountered or resolved the complexities of processing the agent deletion and locative.

Wanat (1971) carried these ideas further by studying the eye movements of adults reading both types of passive sentences. The subjects were not the same as those who had taken part in the EVS study. The eye movements were analyzed for the reading of four agent-included and four agent-deleted passive sentences. The sentences were carefully constructed to be identical in all respects except for the words for the agent of action and the adverb of place:

(1) The boat was piloted by the leader to the pier.

(2) The boat was piloted by the shoals to the pier.

The number of forward fixations and the amount of time spent on forward fixations were the same for both types of passive sentences. However, there were substantially more regressive eye movements when reading the agent-deleted passives and more time was spent on regressions. Furthermore, most regressions occurred *after* the reader had gone through the adverbial by-phrase. This finding explains why the EVS is shortest when the voice reaches the critical word rather than three words antecedent to the agent or adverb. In other words, readers complete the "by + adverb" phrase and then look back in the text, a sequence of activities that narrows the span between the voice and the eyes.

An excellent and informative study by Zollinger (1974) probably should be discussed under the "meaning" rubric, though its relevance to grammar highlights how indistinct the boundary is between syntax and semantics. The normal intonation pattern in English involves stress on the final lexical item (content word) in the clause. This stress pattern becomes obvious by contrasting it with a sentence in which a word other than the final one is stressed:

(1) JOHN climbed the fence yesterday.

(2) John climbed the FENCE yesterday.

Sentence (1) answers the question of who climbed the fence, whereas (2) provides a response to what John climbed. Zollinger argued that the stress pattern carries one or another meaning depending upon what the speaker intends to focus information. This interpretation becomes clearer with additional examples.

(3) Did JOHN put the book on the table?

(4) Did John put the BOOK on the table?

In (3) John is the focus of information, and in (4) book is highlighted. Linguists are uncertain whether focus exists in the underlying meaning of the sentence, which results in the stress placement at the surface level, or whether focus is a surface phenomenon, since the underlying structures for (3) and (4) are the same.

Be that as it may, Zollinger used the phenomenon of contrastive stress in an EVS experiment to test whether the various stress placements are available to readers, that is, will they affect the EVSs differently? Since a major function of the eyes moving ahead of the voice in oral reading is to inform the reader about how to intone the sentence, the use of the EVS methodology to study stress is an ideal marriage of problem and method.

Zollinger's subjects were 72 children, 24 each at the fourth-, fifth-, and sixth-grade levels. The children read 56 frames, consisting of five sentences each. There was one light-out position in each frame. "Four different conditions of information focus were studied in these frames: Focus on the subject; focus on the verb; focus on the direct object; and finally, what is assumed to be a normal intonation condition, focus on the last lexical item of the clause" (p. 39). Examples of each type of frame are presented in figure 8.12.

For example, if the change in information focus were in the subject, the paired target and stimulus sentences would read:

Did *the brave cowboy* shoot two thieves with smoking guns?
No *thin dangerous Sally* shot the bad men with guns.

The assumption being that faced with the stimulus sentence the reader would assume normal intonation and his response would correspond to the supposition that the brave cowboy shot the thieves with something. Furthermore, on reading "No," the reader would assume that he shot the thieves with *something else, not that* someone else had shot the two thieves. (p. 40)

The researcher hypothesized that the EVSs would be shorter in the three stress conditions than in the normal, final item, intonation. The findings were in line with the hypotheses (see figure 8.13). The EVSs were longest when stress occurred in the normal, final lexical position, at every grade level. In the sixth grade there was a large difference between the verb and object conditions. For all grades the largest difference in EVSs was between the subject and final position.

Focus on the subject

TELEVISION STARS HAVE MANY EXCITING ADVENTURES.

HAS KERMIT THE FROG FOOLED BIG BIRD WITH A RUBBER SNAKE?

NO THE GREEN PUPPET FOOLED BIG BIRD WITH A WRINKLED LIZARD.

DID THE BRAVE COWBOY SHOOT TWO THIEVES WITH SMOKING GUNS?

NO THIN* DANGEROUS SALLY SHOT THE BAD MEN WITH GUNS.

Focus on the verb

BOY SCOUTS ENJOY EATING GOOD FOOD AT PICNICS.

WILL HUNGRY BOY SCOUTS FRY HAMBURGERS FOR THEIR DINNER?

NO THE* HUNGRY SCOUTS ATE RAW MEAT FOR THEIR MEAL.

HAVE UNSELFISH DEN FATHERS SHARED THEIR FOOD WITH STARVING BOYS?

NO THE KINDLY FATHERS GAVE THEIR FOOD TO THE BIRDS.

Focus on the direct object

DOCTORS AND NURSES TAKE CARE OF VERY SICK PEOPLE.

DOES THE CAREFUL DOCTOR FIX THE BOY'S WOUNDED ARM?

NO THE UNDERSTANDING MAN CAREFULLY FIXED HIS BROKEN TOE.

HAS THE PLEASANT NURSE JANE GIVEN A SHOT TO CRYING JOHN?

NO THE* KINDLY NURSE GIVES LOLLIPOPS TO ALL SAD CHILDREN.

Focus of the final lexical item

PULLING A RABBIT OUT OF A HAT IS DIFFICULT.

WILL THIN SMILING JOHN SHOW MAGIC TRICKS TO HIS MOTHER?

NO THE HAPPY BOY WILL DO TRICKS FOR HIS FRIENDS.

CAN BOYS AND GIRLS PULL RABBITS OUT OF THE AIR?

NO MOST* CLEVER CHILDREN PULL RABBITS OUT OF BLACK HATS.

Filler

COOKING IS FUN BUT LICKING BOWLS IS BETTER.

WILL CAREFUL YOUNG COOKS MAKE COOKIES FOR THEIR MOTHERS?

NO THE GOOD COOKS LIKE TO MAKE COOKIES FOR THEIR CLASS.

HAS KINDLY GRANDMOTHER SMITH* FROSTED THE TASTY CAKE FOR BILLY?

NO THE NICE OLD WOMAN ICED THE CAKE FOR HIS BROTHER.

*...represents light out position.

8.12
Examples of thematic sentence
frames (Zollinger 1974).

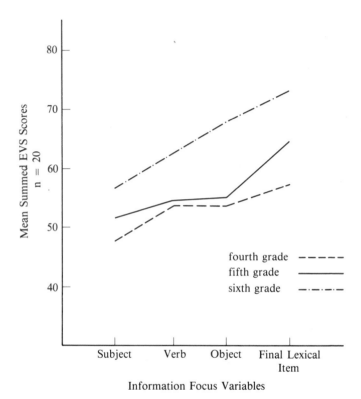

8.13
Mean EVSs of fourth-, fifth-,
and sixth-grade readers, by critical position (Zollinger 1974).

What do these findings mean? As can be seen in figure
8.13, all sentences were of the form: subject-verb-object.
The light-out critical position was after the second word in
the sentence, in the area of the subject. The question-answer
sequence of the critical sentence couplet was designed to

create problems of understanding the sentence in either the areas of the subject, verb, or object. The normal final stress pattern meant the usual interpretation of the sentence. As we saw in chapter 7, points in the text that are difficult to understand result in shortened EVSs. Therefore, the distance into the sentence where the turbulence of comprehension occurred accurately predicts the size of the EVS. It is the genius of this experiment that conceptual difficulty involved the eyes and the voice, yet the general principle holds: EVSs are short at points in the text that are difficult to understand.

The research presented in this chapter is the strongest evidence we have that the size of the EVS is determined in large part by the grammar and meaning of the text. EVSs are longest where constraints are highest. And by extension we believe that all reading follows this generalization. The mediators are presumably the patterns of eye movements regulated by the reader to take advantage of the highest order invariants in the text appropriate to the reader's purposes. Such a view shows reading to be an efficient, flexible, and adaptive process.

NOTES

Note to Chapter 1
1. The discussion of reading is covered in detail in Gibson and Levin (1975).

Note to Chapter 4
1. See Gibson and Levin 1975, ch. 6 for a discussion of Japanese writing.

Notes to Chapter 5
1. The sixth-grade children were deviant on all measures. They were the first subjects tested and were an unselected sample from a rural school. They read poorly for sixth graders. The grade is omitted from subsequent analyses.

2. Several exigencies of this experiment make us cautious about the lack of correlation between instructions and rate and suggest that such reasonable findings may occur in experiments that do not suffer these fortuitous conditions. A mechanical failure gave us no results of reading rate for the eleventh grade. Some children repeated parts of sentences,

spoke to the experimenter while the timer ran, or occasionally omitted responses.

Notes to Chapter 7

1. This use of "information" may be confusing. It is used as in information theory to indicate independent information so that a passage of high constraint yields little new information. To take a simple example, in the sequence of letters *qu* in English orthography, the letter *u* is completely constrained by the preceding *q* and so yields no independent information to that provided by *q*. See, for example, Garner (1962).

2. General usage in the area of reading research now has come to assign the meaning of "decoding" to the translation of spelling to sound, usually by beginning readers. We would use "reading" in the quotation.

Notes to Chapter 8

1. It should be noted that we are considering positions in phrases not sentences, so these findings are not comparable to Buswell's or Fairbanks's.

2. See ch. 5, n. 1.

REFERENCES

Aborn, M., Rubenstein, H., and Sterling, T. D. 1959. Sources of contextual constraint upon words in sentences. *Journal of Experimental Psychology, 57,* 171–80.

Ai, J. W. 1950. A report on psychological studies of the Chinese language in the past three decades. *The Journal of Genetic Psychology, 76,* 207–220.

Anderson, I. H. 1937. Studies in the eye movements of good and poor readers. *Psychological Monographs, 48,* no. 3, 1–35.

Anderson, I. H., and Dearborn, W. F. 1952. *The psychology of teaching reading.* New York: The Ronald Press.

Anderson, I. H., and Swanson, D. E. 1937. Common factors in eye movements in silent and oral reading. *Psychological Monographs, 48,* no. 3, 61–69.

Blumenthal, A. L. 1967. Prompted recall of sentences. *Journal of Verbal Learning and Verbal Behavior, 6,* 203–206.

Bond, G. L., and Tinker, M. A. 1973. *Reading difficulties—their diagnosis and correction.* New York: Appleton-Century-Crofts.

Book, W. F. 1908. *The psychology of skill.* Missoula: University of Montana.

Bouma, H., and deVoogd, A. H. 1974. On the control of eye saccades in reading. *Vision Research, 14,* 273–284.

Bryan, W. L., and Harter, N. 1897. Studies in the physiology and psychology of the telegraphic language. *Psychological Review, 4,* no. 1 (Jan.), 27–53.

————. 1899. Studies on the telegraphic language: the acquisition of a hierarchy of habits. *Psychological Review, 6,* no. 4 (July), 345–375.

Buswell, G. T. 1920. An experimental study of the eye-voice span in reading. *Supplementary Educational Monographs,* no. 17.

————. 1921. The relationship between eye perception and voice response in reading. *Journal of Educational Psychology, 12,* 217–227.

————. 1922. Fundamental reading habits: A study of their development. *Supplementary Educational Monographs,* no. 21.

————. 1927. A laboratory study of the reading of modern foreign languages. *Publications of the American and Canadian Committees on Modern Languages,* vol. 2. New York: The Macmillan Co.

————. 1937. How adults read. *Supplementary Educational Monographs,* no. 45.

Butsch, R. L. C. 1932. Eye movements and the eye-hand span in typewriting. *Journal of Educational Psychology, 23,* no. 2, 104–121.

Cattell, J. M. 1886. The time it takes to see and name objects. *Mind, 11,* 63–65.

Chafe, W. L. 1970. *Meaning and the structure of language.* Chicago: University of Chicago Press.

Chomsky, N. *Aspects of the theory of syntax.* 1965. Cambridge, Mass.: The MIT Press.

Clark, H. H. 1965. Some structural properties of simple active and passive sentences. *Journal of Verbal Learning and Verbal Behavior, 4,* 365–370.

————. 1966. The prediction of recall patterns in simple active sentences. *Journal of Verbal Learning and Verbal Behavior, 5,* 99–106.

Clark, L. A. 1972. Eye-voice span in reading Japanese: a pilot study. Unpublished paper, Cornell University, Ithaca, N.Y., August.

Clark, S. H. 1901. *How to teach reading in the public schools.* Chicago: Scott, Foresman & Co.

————. 1915. *Interpretation of the printed page.* Chicago: Row, Peterson.

Cole, L. 1938. *The improvement of reading.* New York: Farrar and Rinehart, Inc.

Fairbanks, G. 1937. The relation between eye movements and voice in the oral reading of good and poor silent readers. *Psychological Monographs, 48,* no. 3, 78–107.

Fodor, J. A., and Bever, T. G. 1965. The psychological reality of linguistic segments. *Journal of Verbal Learning and Verbal Behavior, 4,* 414–420.

Garner, W. R. 1962. *Uncertainty and structure as psychological concepts.* New York: John Wiley.

Geyer, J. J. 1966. Perceptual systems in reading: a temporal eye-voice span constant. Ph.D. thesis, University of California, Berkeley.

Geyer, J. J. 1969. Perceptual systems in reading: the prediction of a temporal eye-voice span. In *Perception and reading,* ed. H. K. Smith. Newark, Del.: International Reading Association.

Gibson, E. J., and Levin, H. 1975. *The psychology of reading.* Cambridge, Mass.: The MIT Press.

Gladney, T. A., and Kralee, E. E. 1967. The influence of syntactic errors on sentence recognition. *Journal of Verbal Learning and Verbal Behavior, 6,* 692–698.

Gray, C. T. 1917. Types of reading ability as exhibited through tests and laboratory experiments. *Supplementary Educational Monographs,* vol. 1, no. 5.

Gray, W. S. 1916. A study of the emphasis on various phases of reading instruction in two cities. *The Elementary School Journal, 17,* no. 3, 178–186.

———. 1925. Summary of investigations relating to reading. *Supplementary Educational Monographs,* no. 28.

———. 1958. *The teaching of reading and writing.* Chicago: UNESCO, Scott, Foresman & Co.

Grossman, J. K. 1969. Constraints and the EVS in right and

left embedded sentences: a developmental study. Master's dissertation, Cornell University, Ithaca, N.Y.

Hershman, R. L., and Hillix, W. A. 1965. Data processing in typing: typing rate as a function of kind of material and amount exposed. *Human Factors, 7,* 483–492.

Hu, I. 1928. *An experimental study of the reading habits of adult Chinese.* Ph.D. dissertation, the University of Chicago.

Huey, E. B. 1898. Preliminary experiments in the physiology and psychology of reading. *American Journal of Psychology, 9,* no. 4 (July), 575–586.

————. 1908. *The psychology and pedagogy of reading.* New York: Macmillan. Republished by The MIT Press, Cambridge, Mass., 1968.

Jacobsen, O. I. 1941–1942. An experimental study of eye movements in reading vocal and instrumental music. *The Journal of Musicology, 3,* 1–32, 69–100, 133–164, 197–221, 223–226.

Jones, E. E., and Lockhart, A. V. 1919. A study of oral and silent reading in the elementary schools of Evanston. *School and Society, 10,* no. 225, 587–590.

Judd, C. H. 1916. Measuring the work of the public schools. *Cleveland Education Survey,* no. 10. Cleveland, Ohio: Survey Committee of the Cleveland Foundation.

————. 1918. Reading: its nature and development. *Supplementary Educational Monographs,* no. 10.

Judd, C. H., and Buswell, G. T. 1922. Silent reading: a study of the various types. *Supplementary Educational Monographs,* no. 23.

Katz, J. J. 1966. *The philosophy of language.* New York: Harper and Row.

Kolers, P. A. 1970. Three stages of reading. In *Basic studies on reading,* eds. H. Levin and J. P. Williams, pp. 90–118. New York: Basic Books.

Lawson, E. A. 1961. A note on the influence of different orders of approximation to the English language upon eye-voice span. *Quarterly Journal of Experimental Psychology, 13,* no. 1, 53–55.

Levin, H., and Cohn, J. A. 1968. Studies of oral reading: the effects of instructions on the eye-voice span. In *The analysis of reading skill,* eds. H. Levin, E. J. Gibson, and J. J. Gibson, pp. 254–283. Final report, Project No. 5–1213, from Cornell University to the U.S. Office of Education, December.

Levin, H., Ford, B. L., and Beckwith, M. 1968. Homographs in grammatical frames. In *The analysis of reading skill,* eds. H. Levin, E. J. Gibson, and J. J. Gibson, pp. 157–167. Final report, Project No. 5–1213, from Cornell University to the U.S. Office of Education, December.

Levin, H., Grossman, J., Kaplan, E., and Yang, R. 1972. Constraints and the EVS in right and left embedded sentences. *Language and Speech, 15,* no. 1, 30–39.

Levin, H., and Jones, D. 1968. Filled inter-word spaces and the eye-voice span. In *The analysis of reading skill,* eds. H. Levin, E. J. Gibson, and J. J. Gibson, pp. 284–302. Final report, Project No. 5–1213, from Cornell University to the U.S. Office of Education, December.

Levin, H., and Kaplan, E. L. 1968. EVS within active and passive sentences. *Language and Speech, 11,* 251–258.

Levin, H., and Turner, E. A. 1968. Sentence structure and the eye-voice span. In *The analysis of reading skill*, eds. H. Levin, E. J. Gibson, and J. J. Gibson, pp. 196–220. Final report, Project No. 5–1213 from Cornell University to the U.S. Office of Education, December.

McConkie, G., and Rayner, K. 1975. The span of the effective stimulus during a fixation in reading. *Perception and Psychophysics, 17* (June), 578–580.

McDade, J. E. 1941. *Essentials of non-oral beginning reading*. Chicago: The Plymouth Press.

McNeill, D. A., and Lindig, K. 1973. The perceptual reality of phonemes, syllables, words and sentences. *Journal of Verbal Learning and Verbal Behavior, 12,* 419–430.

Mead, C. D. 1915. Silent versus oral reading with one hundred sixth-grade children. *The Journal of Educational Psychology, 6,* no. 6, 345–348.

―――. 1917. Results in silent versus oral reading. *Journal of Educational Psychology, 8,* no. 6, 367–368.

Miller, G. A. 1963. *Language and communication*. New York: McGraw-Hill Book Company. (First ed. 1951)

Miller, G. R., and Coleman, E. B. 1967. A set of thirty-six prose passages calibrated for complexity. *Journal of Verbal Learning and Verbal Behavior, 6,* 851–854.

Morton, J. 1964a. The effects of context on the visual duration threshold for words. *British Journal of Psychology, 55,* no. 2, 165–180.

―――. 1964b. The effects of context upon speed of reading, eye movements and eye-voice span. *Quarterly Journal of Experimental Psychology, 16,* no. 4, 340–354.

Oberholtzer, E. E. 1915. Testing the efficiency in reading in the grades. *The Elementary School Journal, 15,* no. 6, 313–322.

O'Brien, J. A. 1926. *Reading, its psychology and pedagogy,* New York: The Century Company.

Pintner, R. 1913. Oral and silent reading of fourth-grade pupils. *Journal of Educational Psychology, 4,* no. 6, 333–337.

Pintner, R., and Gilliland, A. R. 1916. Oral and silent reading. *Journal of Educational Psychology, 7,* no. 4, 201–212.

Poulton, E. C., and Brown, C. H. 1967. Memory after reading aloud and reading silently. *British Journal of Psychology, 58,* 219–222.

Quantz, J. O. 1897. Problems in the psychology of reading. *Psychological Monographs,* no. 2.

Resnick, L. B. 1970. Relations between perceptual and syntactic control in oral reading. *Journal of Educational Psychology, 61,* no. 5, 382–385.

Rode, S. 1974–1975. Development of phrase and clause boundary reading in children. *Reading Research Quarterly, 10,* no. 1, 124–142.

Rogers, M. V. 1937. Comprehension in oral and silent reading. *Journal of General Psychology, 17,* 394–397.

Sawyer, D. J. 1971. Intra-sentence grammatical constraints in readers' sampling of the visual display. Ph.D. dissertation, Cornell University, Ithaca, N.Y.

Schlesinger, I. M. 1968. *Sentence structure and the reading process.* The Hague: Mouton.

Schmidt, W. A. 1917. An experimental study in the psychology of reading. *Supplementary Educational Monographs*, no. 2.

Shaffer, L. H., and Hardwick, J. 1968. Typing performance as a function of text. *Quarterly Journal of Experimental Psychology*, *20*, 360–369.

———. 1969. Reading and typing. *Journal of Experimental Psychology*, *21*, 381–383.

Sloboda, J. A. 1974a. The eye-hand span: an approach to the study of sight-reading. *Psychology of Music*, *2*, no. 2, 4–10.

———. 1974b. Music reading and prose reading: some comparisons of underlying perceptual processes. Ph.D. dissertation, London University, London, England.

———. 1977. Phrase units as determinants of visual processing in music reading. *British Journal of Psychology*, *68*, 117–124.

Smith, F. 1971. *Understanding reading*. New York: Holt, Rinehart, and Winston.

Stone, C. R. 1922. *Silent and oral reading*. Boston: Houghton Mifflin Co.

Swanson, D. E. 1937. Common elements in silent and oral reading. *Psychological Monographs*, *48*, no. 3, 36–60.

Taylor, W. L. 1953. Cloze procedure: a new tool for measuring readability. *Journalism Quarterly*, *30*, 415.

Thorndike, R. L. 1973. *Reading comprehension: education in fifteen countries*. New York: John Wiley.

Tiffin, J. 1934. Scientific apparatus and laboratory methods:

simultaneous records of eye movements and the voice in oral reading. *Science, 80,* no. 2080, 430–431.

Tiffin, J., and Fairbanks, G. 1937. An eye-voice camera for clinical and research studies. *Psychological Monographs, 48,* 70–77.

Tinker, M. A. 1965. *Bases for effective reading.* Minneapolis: University of Minnesota Press.

Tulving, E., and Gold, C. 1963. Stimulus information and contextual information as determinants of tachistoscopic recognition of words. *Journal of Experimental Psychology, 66,* 319–327.

Vazquez, C. A., Glucksberg, S., and Danks, J. H. 1977–1978. Integration of clauses in oral reading: the effects of syntactic and semantic constraints on the eye-voice span. *Reading Research Quarterly, 13,* no. 2, 174–187.

Vernon, M. D. 1931. *The experimental study of reading.* London: Cambridge University Press.

Wanat, S. F. 1971. *Linguistic structure and visual attention in reading.* Newark, Del.: The International Reading Association Research Reports.

Wanat, S. F., and Levin, H. 1968. The eye-voice span: Reading efficiency and syntactic predictability. In *The analysis of reading skill,* eds. H. Levin, E. J. Gibson, and J. J. Gibson, pp. 237–253. Final report, Project No. 5–1213, from Cornell University to the U.S. Office of Education, December.

Weber, R. M. 1970. First graders' use of grammatical context in reading. In *Basic studies on reading,* eds. H. Levin and J. P. Williams, pp. 147–163. New York: Basic Books.

Woodworth, R. S. 1938. *Experimental psychology*. New York: Henry Holt.

Woodworth, R. S., and Schlosberg, H. 1954. *Experimental Psychology*. New York: Holt, Rinehart, and Winston.

Woody, C. 1922. The effectiveness of oral versus silent reading in the initial memorization of poems. *Journal of Educational Psychology, 13*, no. 8, 477–483.

Zollinger, R. H. 1974. The psychological reality of information focus for the reader. Ph.D. dissertation, Case Western Reserve University, Cleveland, Ohio.

NAME INDEX

Numbers in italics refer to references.

Aborn, M., 87, 94, *151*
Ai, J. W., 22, 25, *151*
Anderson, I. H., 20, 27–28, 31, 36, 38, 48, 57–58, 61, 67, 85, *151*

Beckwith, M., 83, 87–88, *156*
Bever, T. G., 97, *154*
Blumenthal, A. L., 97, *151*
Bond, G. L., 16, 21, *152*
Book, W. F., 71–72, *152*
Bouma, H., 32, *152*
Brown, C. H., 36, *158*
Bryan, W. L., 69–71, *152*
Buswell, G. T., 1, 11, 12 (fig.), 15, 20, 21, 26, 29, 30–31, 32, 33, 36, 38, 40, 47–48, 49 (fig.), 52, 53–54, 57, 62–64, 65, 83–85, 89, 90, 93–94, 94–95, 96, 97, 104, 138, 150n, *152, 155*
Butsch, R. L. C., 72–73, *153*

Cattell, J. M., 83, *153*
Chafe, W. L., 135, *153*
Chomsky, N., 86, 140, *153*
Clark, H. H., 115–117, 121, *153*
Clark, S. H., 21, 82–83, *153*
Clarke, L. A., 45–46, 91, *153*
Cohn, J. A., 50, 56, 58–61, *156*
Cole, L., 20, 25, 31, 36, *153*
Coleman, E. B., 94, *157*

Danks, J., 103, 107 (fig.), 108, 110, 111, 114, 139, *160*
Dearborn, W. F., 20, 38, 40, 48, 67, 85, 96, *151*
deVoogd, A. H., 32, *152*

Fairbanks, G., 13, 20, 41, 65–66, 90–91, 95–96, 97, 104, 150n, *153, 160*
Fodor, J. A., 97, *154*
Ford, B. L., 83, 87–88, *156*

Garner, W. R., 127, 150n, *154*
Geyer, J. J., 13, 14, 66–67, 89–90, *154*
Gibson, E. J., 21, 65, 149n, *154*
Gilliland, A. R., 24–26, 34, *158*
Gladney, T. A., 135, *154*
Glucksberg, S., 103, 107 (fig.), 108, 110, 111, 114, 139, *160*
Gold, C., 87
Gray, C. T., 8–11, 57, 62, 72, 83, *154*
Gray, W. S., 21, 22–24, 25, 26, 27, 29, 32, 33, 36, 43, *154*
Grossman, J. K., 113, 123, 126–132, *154, 156*

Hardwick, J., 75, *159*
Harter, N., 69–71, *152*
Hershman, R. L., 73–75, *155*
Hillex, W. A., 73–75, *155*
Hu, I., *155*
Huey, E. B., 1, 8, 33, 40, 83, *155*

Jacobsen, O. I., 76–77, *155*
Jones, D., 41–43, 110–113, 123–125, *156*
Jones, E. E., 28, 35, *155*
Judd, C. H., 20, 20–21, 25, 29, 31, 33, 36, 57, *155*

Kaplan, E. L., 3, 16, 42, 91–92, 98, 103, 117–122, 123–125, 126–132, 133, *156*
Katz, J. J., 140, *156*
Kolers, P. A., 87, 94, 104, 138, *156*
Kralee, E. E., 135, *154*

Lawson, E. A., 16, 44, 92, *156*
Levin, H., 3, 15, 16, 21, 41–43, 48, 50, 51, 55, 56, 58–61, 65, 83, 87–88, 91–92, 98–103,

104–108, 110–113, 115, 117–133, 139, 140–142, 149n, *154, 156, 157, 160*
Lindig, K, *157*
Lockhart, A. V., 28, 35, *155*

McConkie, G., 4, *157*
McDade, J. E., 27
McNeill, D. A., *157*
Mead, C. D., 34, *157*
Miller, G. A., 91–92, *157*
Miller, G. R., 94, *157*
Morton, J., 14, 15 (fig.), 44, 54–55, 87, 92, *157*

Oberholzer, E. E., 25, *157*
O'Brien, J. A., 29, 36, 41, 64, *158*

Pinter, R., 24–26, 34, *158*
Poulton, E. C., 36, *158*

Quantz, J. O., 1, 7–8, 33, 39, 40, 53, 83, 93, 96, *158*

Rayner, K., 4, *157*
Resnick, L. B., 16, 43, 50, 51, 103, *158*
Rode, S., 15, 50, 51, 52, 98, 103, 108, 112–115, 138, 139, *158*
Rogers, M. V., 20, 36, *158*
Rubinstein, H., 87, 94, *151*

Sawyer, D. J., 135, 137, *158*
Schlesinger, I. M., 16, 43–45, 55, 92, 98, 103, 139, *158*
Schlosberg, H., 67, 86, *160*
Schmidt, W. A., 29, 33–34, *158*
Shaffer, L. H., 75, *159*
Sloboda, J. A., 77–79, *159*
Smith, F., 30–31, 37, 67, *159*
Sterling, T. D., 87, 94, *151*

Stone, C. R., 25, 26, 27, 29, 36,
    159
Swanson, D. E., 20, 27–28, 31,
    36, *151, 159*

Taylor, W. L., 126, *159*
Thorndike, R. L., 43, *159*
Tiffin, J., 11, 13, *159–160*
Tinker, M. A., 16, 21, 32, 41, 48,
    86, *152, 160*
Tulving, E., 87
Turner, E. A., 15, 48, 51, 55, 56,
    98–103, 104–108, 113, 115,
    122–125, 139, *157*

Vazquez, C. A., 103, 107 (fig.),
    108, 110, 111, 114, 139, *160*
Vernon, M. D., 41, 57, 64, 85, 96

Wanat, S. F., 22, 29, 30, 33,
    133–134, 136 (fig.), 140–142,
    160
Weber, R. M., 52, 104, 138, *160*
Woodworth, R. S., 1, 67, 69, 75,
    86, *160*
Woody, C., 35, *160*

Yang, R., 126–132, *156*

Zollinger, R. H., 50, 142–147,
    160

SUBJECT INDEX

Age, 2, 24–27, 31, 39, 47–52. *See*
    also Children
    effects of on EVS, 47–51
    and reading to phrase bound-
        aries, 51–52
Arabic, 24
Articulation, 36
    rate of, 28, 60, 64–65
Attention spans, 31, 65, 67

Bimodality practice, 37
Burmese, 23

Children, 25–27, 48–49, 53–54,
    122–123, 138–139, 144. *See*
    also Developmental studies
    embedded constraints and, 132
    memory studies and, 34
    passive sentence constraints
        and, 113–115
    unitizing function of grammar
        and, 114, 123–135
Chinese, 22–23

Clause, 114
Comprehension, 34–40, 57, 64.
    See also Memory
    oral, 27
    silent, 27
    sound and, 25–35
Context, 87
Contextual constraints, 54
Critical position, 2, 104, 111, 115

Developmental studies, 24–27,
    48–51, 62–63. *See also* Age;
    Children
Dictaphone, Edison, 9

Ear-hand span, 70–71, 73, 75, 76
Electrooculography, 14, 19
English, 23, 54, 81–82, 92
Experimental Psychology, 1
Eye-hand span, 71–75, 76, 77–79
Eye movement, 2, 16–17, 29–31,
    33, 38, 86, 133–137
    EVS and, 88–91

Eye movement (continued)
  music and, 77
  reading rate and, 26, 67
  regressive, 21–24, 26, 29, 57, 64,
    66, 88, 90, 133, 142
  regularity of, 26–27, 30, 57
  silent vs. oral reading, 32
  studies of, 58–60, 88–91
  text constraints and, 88–89
  text difficulty and, 56–57
  typewriting and, 72–73
Eye-performance span, 76–77
Eye-voice lead, 41
Eye-voice separation, 7, 62,
  91–92, 95

French, 23

German, 43
Gilbert eye movement camera,
  13
Grammar, 86–88, 103–104. See
  also Grammatical structure
Grammatical constraints, 132.
  See also Grammatical structure
Grammatical phrases, 98–108
  length of, 110–113
Grammatical structure, 41, 82,
  87–88, 91, 96, 97, 108–109,
  114, 137, 138–139
Gray's Oral Reading Paragraph,
  62

Hebrew, 24, 43–46, 92, 98, 103
Homographs, 83–84, 87–88

Idea, 38, 39, 61. See also Meaning unit
Instructions, 56–61

Intrasentence constraints, 93,
  115, 121
Iowa Silent Reading Test, 27,
  65–66

Japanese, 45–46, 91

Korean, 23

Language, 139–140
  meaning of, 31, 32, 37, 41, 138–
  139
Languages, 43–46, 85
  comparison of visual fixations
    among, 23–34
Line position, 39–41, 96, 111
Lip movement, 21, 33
Locative forms, 30

Meaning. See Language, meaning of
Meaning unit, 81, 96, 97, 138. See
  also Idea
Memory, 34–40, 65
  oral tests of, 37
  short-term, 89
  studies of, 34
  typewriting and, 74–75
  Musculature, 19, 34
  speech, 19, 33–34
  vocal, 33
Music, 76–79

Noun phrase, 113–115. See also
  Phrase boundary

Orthography, 43

Passives, 101. See also Sentence,
  passive

Passives (continued)
  agent-deleted, 22, 30, 140–142
Perception accuracy, 28–29, 38
Photography, eye-movement,
  13–14
Phrase. *See* Grammatical
  phrase; Noun phrase; Verb
  phrase
Phrase boundary, 97–98, 101–
  102
  effects of age and, 51–52
  in music, 77–78
  and span, 55, 111
Poetry, 23
  memorizing of, 34–35
*Psychology and Pedagogy of
  Reading, The,* 1

Reading, 4
  boundary *vs.* nonboundary,
    102–103
  educational diagnosis of, 2
  errors, 103–104
  grammar and, 137
  materials, 2
  motor theory of, 40
  oral vs. silent, 8, 19–20, 29, 38
  phrase units and, 21
  process of, 3–5, 6, 60–61
  rate, 26, 33–34, 40, 52–56, 60,
    62–64
  skill, 26–27, 36, 38, 62–69, 85
  speech units and, 21
  speed, 64–65
  styles of, 56
  thought units and, 21
  "Reading value," 24–25
Regression. *See* Eye movement,
  regressive

Saccade length, 26, 88

Semantics, 138–147. *See also*
  Language, meaning of
Sentence, 92–97; active 22,
  111–113, 115–126
  deep vs. surface structure of a,
    139–140
  end constraints of a, 112
  left-embedded, 29, 30, 126–127
  passive, 22, 29, 112, 115–126,
    133, 140–142
  right-embedded, 29, 30, 125–137
  types of, 22, 30, 98–101, 115
Serbo-Croatian, 43

Telegraphy, 69–71, 75–76, 79.
  See also Ear-hand span
Text, 2, 24, 29–30, 38, 81–85,
  135–137
  constraints in, 88, 109
  difficulty of, 56–57, 89–90
  grammatical and semantic char-
    acteristics of, 17, 86–88, 109
  memory for, 34, 38, 74–75
  nature of, 20–24
  readability of, 84–86
  "syntactic-semantic" charac-
    teristics of, 24, 135, 147
  typewriting and, 73–75
Thought, 82. *See also* Idea
  units of, 39, 64, 67, 97, 138
Typewriting, 71–76, 79. *See also*
  Eye-hand span
Typography, 2, 20, 41–43
  artifacts of, 94

Verb phrase, 113–115

Watsonian dictum, 65
Writing systems, 23–24, 43–46
  ideographic, 23, 45–46